CW01085120

Sissinghurst

THE DREAM GARDEN

Sissinghurst
THE DREAM GARDEN

Tim Richardson

Foreword by Dan Pearson
Photography by Jason Ingram

FRANCES
LINCOLN

This book is dedicated to Claire, my wife

First published in 2020 by Frances Lincoln,
an imprint of The Quarto Group.
The Old Brewery, 6 Blundell Street
London, N7 9BH,
United Kingdom
T (0)20 7700 6700
www.QuartoKnows.com

Text © 2020 Tim Richardson
Images © 2020 Jason Ingram, except where listed on page 223
Copyright © The Quarto Group 2020

Tim Richardson has asserted his moral right to be identified
as the Author of this Work in accordance with the Copyright
Designs and Patents Act 1988.

All rights reserved. No part of this book may be reproduced or
utilized in any form or by any means, electronic or mechanical,
including photocopying, recording or by any information storage
and retrieval system, without permission in writing from
Frances Lincoln.

Every effort has been made to trace the copyright holders of
material quoted in this book. If application is made in writing
to the publisher, any omissions will be included in future editions.

A catalogue record for this book is available from the
British Library.

ISBN 978 0 7112 3734 6
Ebook ISBN 978 0 7112 6163 1

10 9 8 7 6 5 4 3

Editorial Director: Helen Griffin
Designer: Rachel Cross
Copy editor: Sarah Higgens
Project editor: Zia Allaway
Photography: Jason Ingram
Illustrations: Nicky Cooney
Illustration retouching: Robbie Polley
Proofreader: Joanna Chisholm
Indexer: Michele Moody

Printed in China

Brimming with creative inspiration, how-to projects and useful information
to enrich your everyday life, Quarto Knows is a favourite destination for those
pursuing their interests and passions. Visit our site and dig deeper with our
books into your area of interest: Quarto Creates, Quarto Cooks, Quarto Homes,
Quarto Lives, Quarto Drives, Quarto Explores, Quarto Gifts, or Quarto Kids.

Contents

Page 1: Alliums and hesperis in the White Garden. Pages 2–3: The Top Courtyard at Sissinghurst Castle, acquired in 1930 by Harold Nicolson and Vita Sackville-West. Left: Lilium regale with corncockle: the exotic with the commonplace, one of Sissinghurst's abiding tensions.

FOREWORD

by Dan Pearson

I have known Sissinghurst and been a regular visitor since I was a boy in the mid seventies. My father would drive the two of us from Hampshire on an annual pilgrimage and we would walk its rarefied enclosures with notebooks in hand in the knowledge that this was somewhere special. I remember from early on the feeling of awe and then a rising disappointment that we would simply never be able to garden at this level and with such rigour, for at that point, and in the decades since, it has been a garden of horticultural excellence with perfection at every turn.

As I started to read Vita Sackville-West's words on gardening in my teens, it became clear that the gardener I had been reading was doing something rather different from the place we walked in person. She was gardening loosely and with the feeling of the place dictating a mood that was free and to a degree decadent. Entire sections of the garden might be allowed to peak for a moment and then be gone, in the knowledge that you could turn your back and refocus elsewhere. The tapestry of polyanthus in the Nuttery, the Rose Garden, or the bulbs of the Lime Walk bloomed for a glorious interlude but were allowed to pass. It was a garden that took you into another world. It was a garden that immersed you. Vita's writings talked of a place that was first and foremost lived in by its owners and where ideas and experiments did not demand year-round perfection. But Sissinghurst *then* did not have the pressures and close scrutiny it has now, having over time become one of the most visited gardens in Britain. Mulleins breaking into the narrow paths could be negotiated, and roses reaching beyond their allocated space were free to reign.

A garden is ultimately the gardener and since Vita's death in 1962 Sissinghurst had become somewhere entirely different. When the National Trust took over, an inevitable tightening up eventually saw the garden reach extraordinary horticultural heights in the hands of Pam Schwerdt and Sibylle Kreutzberger, who crossed over with Vita but went on to make the garden their own and defined a new sense of expectation. The way the garden became was ultimately driven by the need to provide for the public and, in so doing, the sense of place was slowly altered. It was not a garden where you could turn your back when an area had peaked, or walk around a mullein. It was a garden that performed, but at the expense of the magic that came from it being lived in more casually under the guiding eyes of its makers.

In 2014 Troy Scott Smith, then head gardener, invited me to become a godparent to the garden. The role was one I was happy to explore, for there is nothing like getting to know a garden from behind the scenes and through the people that work there. Troy had sent me his manifesto by way of introduction. When he had applied for the role at Sissinghurst, he had talked of the need for change and to the credit of the National Trust they employed him with this vision. He wanted to recapture the sense of place that Vita had celebrated in her writings and in the home that she and Harold Nicolson had made at the castle. A garden that was inextricably linked to the buildings it surrounded and, in turn, the Kentish countryside that swept up to its walls. He saw there being a need for the place to be unlocked from the rigour that had become bound up with the garden's identity since the death of the owners. A challenge perhaps for one of the most famous gardens in the country, but for one with such good bones, a new era of excitement.

Anyone who owns or gardens a garden knows all too well that feeling of only seeing what needs doing. Sometimes it is hard to focus on the achievements or the long view, or to simply take stock and see what is happening in the here and now. My meetings with Troy took a different season every year, with notebooks and open brief to walk and talk and ponder. A second eye from an outsider is often exactly what is needed and we cultivated an openness in the discussion, where opinions may count here but not there, and where the mission is to get to the essence of things. We talked of taking the pressure off the garden and of opening it up again to the land around it. We discussed how best to 'relax' the planting and make it breathe easy. To get back to the spirit of what Vita and Harold had envisioned for the place. It has been a slow and respectful process of change, and an ongoing one now that the garden has been passed on to Michelle Cain in her position as head gardener.

In 2018 Troy asked me to take on the role of reimagining Delos, an area that had lost its way and needed more than a light touch. Vita and Harold had been inspired by a voyage they made to the Greek island in 1935 and sought to recapture its spirit at Sissinghurst. They had made stone walls to reflect the ruggedness of the island and planted a 'wild' place using plants from the region. This must have been a very new approach to making a garden at that point, but they were learning as they gardened and the site they chose by the Priest's House was far from ideal. It faced north, with exposure to the winds from across the fields, and the heavy Weald clay could not have favoured their Mediterranean palette less and the garden ultimately failed.

My godparenting role, and the remaking of Delos, have allowed me to get under the skin of Sissinghurst, but the pages of Tim Richardson's book dig deeper to reveal Vita and Harold's unique relationship through the garden they made together – a relationship that defied convention and manifested itself here in the walls and hedges and the juxtaposition of a very particular informality. It is revealed in their descriptions of the garden and the way they lived in it as a home, a blend of experimentation and daring, and a means of personal expression and partnership. In the fragile and ephemeral world they created, they captured something potent and long-lasting. A vision that has been held in place through words but, most importantly, a vision that has seduced and captivated generations of garden lovers. A garden that by its very nature has been subject to change but one that has a strong enough blueprint to have stood the test of time.

'For there is nothing more potent or better than this:
when a man and a woman, sharing the same ideas about
life, keep house together. It is a thing which causes pain
to their enemies and pleasure to their friends. But only
they themselves know what it really means.'

Homer, *Odyssey*, quoted in *Another World Than This*,
1945, edited by Vita Sackville-West and Harold Nicolson

Introduction

If a garden is to be considered an art form, rather than simply a hobby or pastime, then in the pantheon of British gardens, Sissinghurst might be compared to the *Mona Lisa*. Like the painting, it has become so familiar that it is difficult to appreciate it for what it is: a great garden on its own merits, as opposed to a visitor attraction burdened by an international reputation. That was certainly my feeling when I embarked upon this book; I thought I knew the garden well already. Yet rather to my surprise, the process of getting to know Sissinghurst afresh, and in a far more intense manner than before, has revealed that there is plenty that is new to say. In fact, on occasion, it has felt as if, all this time, the garden has been hiding in plain sight.

A considerable amount of descriptive – if not critical – attention has been lavished on Sissinghurst over the years because this is a place which exerts a hold over people like no other. That sense of connection is in part attributable to the personalities of its makers, Harold Nicolson and Victoria ('Vita') Sackville-West, who acquired Sissinghurst in 1930 and over the ensuing

LEFT: Cecil Beaton's photograph of Vita and Harold in front of their quarters at the South Cottage in 1959.

decades poured so much of themselves into it, without ever descending into exhibitionism. The knowledge that the garden was made by them, for them, and for them alone – despite the presence of so many paying visitors, even in their lifetimes – has paradoxically only served to cement this feeling of intimacy with the visiting public. The couple's unconventional open marriage – they were both essentially homosexual – has also, for some, made this corner of Kent into a site of pilgrimage and fascination. The long-standing horticultural reputation of the garden has resulted in a number of books on Sissinghurst – by Anne Scott-James, Jane Brown, Tony Lord and Adam Nicolson; and on Vita – by Victoria Glendinning, Sarah Raven, Matthew Dennison and Jane Brown (again). All of these publications come highly recommended. Yet my hope is that with this book I have been able to offer something a little different by teasing out the invisible meanings of the garden, which exist alongside its more tangible sensory delights. For gardens are not only a matter of what can be seen, smelled, heard and touched. Just as much, they are about what is felt, what is thought, and the atmosphere of the place. Sissinghurst was conceived in an intensely personal way – with every planting decision by Vita, and every angle and vista designed by Harold, expressive of their innermost emotions, hopes and desires. They put their all into Sissinghurst. It is a place where the character of the creators has somehow endured in its very fabric, where the emotional resonance of the life they lived together persists and seems palpable.

I am not going to make any excuses for the wilful intermixing, in this book, of sturdy horticultural description with biographical detail and speculation regarding Harold and Vita's intellectual and aesthetic motivations. As is so often the case, the garden was not just a hobby for them; it was the life-project of two intellectuals, expressive of their world views, of their unconventional love for each other, and of a passion for the place itself. It also speaks of the cultural context of the times, and of their own engagement with literature and the challenge of what we now call modernism, which inevitably seeped into the garden's pores (and arguably into its structure, too). For Vita, there was no fundamental distinction between writing and gardening as creative activities. She expressed this co-mingling of the disciplines in one of her early poems, simply entitled 'Sonnet' (1921):

My garden all is overblown with roses,
My spirit all is overblown with rhyme,
And like a drunken honeybee I waver
From house to garden and again to house,
And, undetermined which delight to favour,
On verse and rose alternately carouse.

The depth of their interaction with the garden meant that Vita and Harold became virtually one with it as time passed. Perhaps that is why Harold was so devastated after Vita's death in 1962, when embarrassed visitors would find Sissinghurst's elderly owner seated on the Tower Lawn with tears streaming down his cheeks. His 'Viti', as he nicknamed her, was never again going to pad down those steps in the tower. With Vita gone, the garden, and Harold himself, were merely existing in a kind of half-life, for without her, they could never be complete. One of the reasons why the garden speaks to visitors so directly is because people recognise from personal experience this sensation of a shared relationship with a garden – and the sense of loss that can ensue.

Knole

At Sissinghurst, everything begins and everything ends with Knole. The great seat of the Sackville family in west Kent, near Sevenoaks, was given to Vita's ancestors by Queen Elizabeth I in 1566. It was here that Vita spent her childhood, and it was from here that she was exiled after the death of her father in 1928, barred from what she viewed as her rightful inheritance because of her gender. An only child, and neglected by her parents, as a young girl she found herself frequently alone with its 'pictures and galleries and empty rooms', as she put it in her poem 'To Knole' (1917). As Vita 'wandered shoeless in the galleries' of this great house, she role-played her way through history, writing private plays and historical fiction from a precociously early age. This habit of making stories out of places persisted in her; indeed, Sissinghurst can be interpreted as a purpose-built arena for such role playing.

As has been observed several times, not least by Vita, the garden she made with Harold might be understood as an attempt to recreate something akin to her beloved Knole, in the form of a sequence of enclosed spaces reminiscent of the interior of a great house, where each room has its own personality and style. At Knole these would include the Poet's Parlour, the Venetian Ambassador's Bedroom, the Brown Gallery, the Colonnade, the long attics filled with lumber. But Vita did not attempt to recreate these specific room environments at Sissinghurst. Instead, she made a series of distinct and characterful outdoor episodes, where the

'rooms' are furnished with plants, the 'carpets' are made of grass and the 'walls' are clipped yew and hornbeam, while the glorious roses that clothe the walls form a continuous 'picture gallery'. Sissinghurst's status as a partial ruin gave the project an added piquancy in that the deconstructed version of Knole that Vita made for herself reflected her own status as a rejected and stricken would-be chatelaine. She revelled in the ruination of Sissinghurst as 'commensurate with a frustrated dream', as she put it in her poem about the garden.

Meanwhile, in Vita's poem about Knole there is a memorable image of her delight at watching sunbeams pass through an oriel window:

I daily stood and laughing drank the beams,
And, catching fistfuls, pressed them in my mouth.

If Vita wanted to bodily consume Knole, a place she loved more than any human being, then it might be said that at Sissinghurst she somehow expressed its architectural fabric in garden form.

Vita was acutely aware of the history of Knole and the people who had lived there, those 'portraits that I knew so well, they almost spoke'. Clearly, she felt their presence all the time – and continued to do so even when she had moved elsewhere. Yet she did not believe in ghosts and actually became very angry when a local newspaper reported that Sissinghurst was haunted. Vita had no interest in ghosts because the concept of the living past was a forcefully tangible part of her daily experience. As a child she had stalked the darkened corridors of Knole carrying a candle before her, confident that she would encounter nothing supernatural. Because for Vita the past was alive, not dead. She had no need for ghosts because she was a kind of ghost herself. Several people remarked upon her endearing personal quality of seeming to be out of step with the present, a sense that she was an other-worldly being who apparently dwelt in the past. It is not an uncommon trait among the

ABOVE: A corner of the Cottage Garden, with tulips, wallflowers, asphodels and the yellow-flowered shrub Hippocrepis emerus.

aristocracy, though, in Vita's case, it was more marked. This was one of the remarkable qualities that drew Virginia Woolf to Vita, and ultimately led to Virginia's book *Orlando* (1928), her fantastical-biographical study of a gender-shifting, century-hopping aristocrat.

Dreaming

The subtitle of this book is *The Dream Garden* because Sissinghurst operates in a dreamlike way on several levels. To begin with, Sissinghurst seems 'dreamy' to us because of the qualities of intimacy and absorption that have been described above. Something of this was caught by Vita in her novel *Family History*, which contains a description of a garden that is clearly based on Sissinghurst. That novel was published in 1932, the year she and Harold moved in. For the lovers Miles and Evelyn (note the gender-ambiguous name), the garden is a milieu of barely suppressed desire:

ABOVE: Rosa 'Sissinghurst Castle', which Vita 'discovered' and named on her first visit. It was growing on an old apple tree in the Orchard.

They strolled up and down the path under the wall. They forgot the world, and broke off little branches of southernwood [artemisia] to crush between their fingers. The pansies and the white lilies stood out startlingly in the half-light. It was a dream, a suspension, a trance.

Sissinghurst's historical status and its fairy-tale qualities (with the tower looming above) also play in to these feelings of transcendence and escapism. And the focus of this dreamlike experience, where we seem caught between two worlds, between waking and dreaming, between life and death, has to be the White Garden. The poem that serves as an epilogue to this book is intended to be an evocation of these effects.

The garden's dreamlike character arose in part as a result of the strategies of physical disorientation, disintegration and deconstruction that Harold deployed in his apparently illogical ground plan. It was a working method that can be related to contemporary artistic currents, including the stream-of-consciousness device of literary modernism (pioneered by Virginia Woolf), the eclectic and deconstructed form of T.S. Eliot's poetry, the neo-baroque movement of the 1930s, and European surrealism. These matters are discussed later in the book – chiefly in the 'Interlude' between chapters 5 and 6. In the visual arts the fragmentation of the garden's plan might be related to cubism and its surreal qualities to the work of Paul Nash and other contemporary English painters, while the revelry in colour could be aligned with the Fauvist movement (led by Matisse and Derain). Indeed, the sheer sensuous hedonism of Vita's planting can be described as painterly in its effect: a clamour of colours and textures and scents.

Another theme associated with dreaming is that of role playing in the garden, a compulsion that can be applied to Vita especially. She was from the outset attracted to Sissinghurst as an arena for dramatising her multiple selves, immediately referring to herself, as well as the potential garden, as a 'sleeping beauty in the tower'. Each part of the garden, each episode, has its own distinct and private character, as if we are delving into these little worlds for just a few moments.

Finally, the garden seems dreamlike because for Vita and Harold it was a simultaneously portentous and auspicious place that represented their conjoined fate. To them it seemed almost preordained that they would come to Sissinghurst, with the garden both a foretelling and consummation of that destiny. In all of their writings and letters to each other, you never gain the impression that Vita and Harold wished to express absolute dominion over the place, despite their strong feelings of possession. There is a sense that they are conspiring with the garden as a third personality in their relationship. It became inseparable from them. It acted, too, as a kind of nexus and intensification of the mythical (at least to Vita) and vulnerable Kentish landscape that surrounds the ruined castle. For Kent has always seemed fragile and under threat to Kentish people, huddled together on the front line of potential invasion. Vita felt this, particularly, during the Second World War, when the Battle of Britain raged in the skies above and soldiers were posted as lookouts atop Sissinghurst's tower. (The shore-side garden made by Derek Jarman on the shingle at Dungeness is another place that seems expressive of this sense of Kentish vulnerability.)

Perhaps one useful illustration of Vita's feelings can be drawn from these lines in one of her more experimental poems:

Down the long path beneath the garden wall,
She stooped, setting her plants in the winter dusk.
She knew she must make an end of setting her plants,
Though why she must make an end she nothing knew.

This captures something of the irresistible compulsion Vita felt to make a garden, and to continue making it over and over again, without fully knowing why. It is as if she is not really in control (a sensation that will be familiar to all gardeners…) That poem is actually entitled 'A Dream', which again reflects Vita's interest in the subconscious. She made a habit of writing down her dreams, which she later collected as a manuscript known as her 'book of dreams'. And the most potent recurring motif that bubbled up from Vita's subconscious was, of course, Knole.

Trust

The garden was passed to the National Trust in 1967, and when Harold died the following year, his younger son Nigel Nicolson continued to live at Sissinghurst in a custodian role, as a representative of the donor family. Pamela Schwerdt and Sibylle Kreutzberger, the joint head gardeners whom Vita had employed in 1959, continued in their posts, while Graham Stuart Thomas, as chief gardens adviser at the National Trust, found himself in charge of strategic direction.

With hindsight, it might be observed that the Trust would have been hard-pressed to have come up with a group of people who were temperamentally less well suited to maintaining Vita's unbridled style of gardening. 'Pam and Sibylle' – as they were universally known in the gardens world – had trained at Waterperry, a women's horticultural college in Oxfordshire, presided over by the strict matriarch Beatrix Havergal. They were professional gardeners to a tee, schooled in the highest horticultural traditions, where untidiness – let alone unruliness – was seen as a shortcoming to be corrected. Thomas was, if anything, even more of a stickler, as a gardener of almost legendary exactitude who did not brook dissent or slackness of any kind. As for Nicolson, Sarah Raven has commented that 'Nigel liked it kept very tidy' – evidently he was relieved that the garden had been placed in the hands of competent professionals who could, in the view of everyone then in charge, raise the horticultural standard of the garden even higher. There is a revealing comment about Sissinghurst in Thomas's memoir, *Recollections of Great Gardeners* (2003), when he recalled of Vita and Harold: 'They had no horticultural training and when I first saw the borders I was not impressed.' But adopting the attitude that there were mistakes to be corrected and areas to improve at Sissinghurst was to miss something of the character of the garden. Its ramshackle, at times almost shabby, nature was all part of its charm. Arguably what the garden required was not improvement or refreshment or refinement, but simple obeisance to the style and flavour set by Vita in her day: a romantic, chaotic creativity. The tone and feel of Vita's garden was amateurish but in the very best sense, in that her own personality shone through in every planting decision.

The biggest challenge facing the custodians of historic gardens is authenticity – how to conserve, restore or attempt to recreate something of the original character of a place. This becomes even more difficult in gardens where planting has played an important role in the formation of that character – because herbaceous perennials die down each year and shrubs (including roses) will also eventually go. It means that any garden of this kind will not naturally reappear the following season in identical guise; new choices about planting will always have to be made. This issue, which is in some ways insoluble, lies at the root of the problem that Troy Scott Smith, head gardener at Sissinghurst from 2013 until 2019, was brought in to address – and did so with some success.

The paradox of Sissinghurst is that since Harold's death it has always been gardened too well. That sounds odd, perhaps, but even into the early 2010s there continued to be a feeling within the Trust that the garden ought to reflect the professionalism and high standards of the organisation at large. The garden was maintained with reference to a Trust manual dedicated

to '20th-century flower-gardening', as if this was a generic style. But the fact remains, this was always an amateur's garden, in private ownership. It has proven extremely difficult for organisations such as the Trust to replicate the idiosyncratic texture of maintenance that implies. At the same time, it must also be acknowledged that 'conservation philosophy' barely existed in 1967, when the Trust took over the garden, with the influential Garden History Society then in its infancy. In many cases the Trust saw its role as primarily saving a great garden from dereliction and disappearance. That was the main objective at Sissinghurst.

And so it emerged that the attitude of the new custodians of Sissinghurst was rather at variance with Vita's own. For despite her reputation, Vita did not view herself as an expert on gardening. Quite late in life, when Sissinghurst was already famous nationally, if not internationally, she signed up to a gardening course at the Royal Horticultural Society, where she was herself sitting on the governing council. This was not mock humility but an acknowledgment that as a horticulturist she was untrained. Careful reading of her weekly *Observer* columns, which she produced from 1946 to 1961, shows that the advice she dispensed was either hard-won in her own garden as the result of her experiments with specific plant groups, or (more often) a distillation of conversations with specialist nursery owners.

Vita always had professional help, of course, and recognised and admired knowledge, diligence and expertise. She approved of Pam and Sibylle (whom she dubbed 'the *Mädchen*') for their efficient attitude and appearance, and for the way 'they do not stop working when one talks to them.' But even while Vita worked alongside 'the help' on a daily basis, she always remained firmly in control of the garden's tone. Of her earlier head gardener Jack Vass she remarked that 'Vass is a gardener after my own heart, I love his keenness and knowledge, only I think it is a good thing to be behind him to check his love of over-neatness with my own more romantic and more untidy view of what the garden should be.' There lies the essence of the problem: who was going to check on 'over-neatness' once Vita was gone? At the same time, there was a certain method to Vita's horticultural 'madness'. In a lecture she (rather boldly) gave to the RHS in 1951 she stated:

> I see signs, which I welcome, of a rougher and untidier way of treating plants. Let me say, for example, that we are no longer instructed to prune our hybrid Tea Roses to within an inch of the ground: we let them grow up into tall bushes. Let me point out also that we have now taken to the idea of growing certain sorts of Roses as shrubs. The hybrid Musks for example: we let them ramp away; we do not hack at them with the knife or secateurs. They would lose all their character if we did. A judicious (and most convenient) appearance of neglect is therefore what we may look forward to seeing.

Yet this vision of a 'rough and untidy' style of gardening remained anathema to the professional horticulturists who were now looking after the garden, with the best of intentions. As a result, after Vita's death, the garden's character changed decisively. Certain well-documented alterations were made to the built fabric of the garden – such as laying stone paths in place of grass – while the maintenance regime was also 'tightened up' (no more wayward rose stems waving in the air). There was more of an emphasis on making garden episodes which were of interest across the seasons, instead of Vita's unabashed delight in fleeting moments of horticultural intensity: her single-colour, single-species or single-season plantings. The garden became much more complex in terms of the herbaceous perennials on display, and the range of shrubs was extended so that the whole garden was somewhat less focused on the prime rose period of late May to early July. Horticultural standards remained of

the highest under the two head gardeners who followed in the footsteps of Pam and Sibylle (1959–91) and who were both promoted from within, having previously been deputy head gardeners at Sissinghurst: Sarah Cook (1991–2004) and Alexis 'Lex' Datta (2004–13). (Even Troy Scott Smith had had an earlier stint at the garden, in the mid 1990s.) There is certainly an advantage in creating a close-knit team, but there grew a sense that Sissinghurst was operating inside its own bubble.

For some visitors, the garden seemed to have lost something of the old Vita magic over the years. I felt this keenly as I served on the Trust's gardens advisory panel (the voluntary committee on which Vita herself had served). When I aired these matters concerning Sissinghurst in my column in the *Daily Telegraph* in 2004, I felt I was only echoing what many respected gardeners and designers had been saying privately for some time.

ABOVE: Branches covered with apple blossom flowering in spring in the Orchard, with the tower beyond.

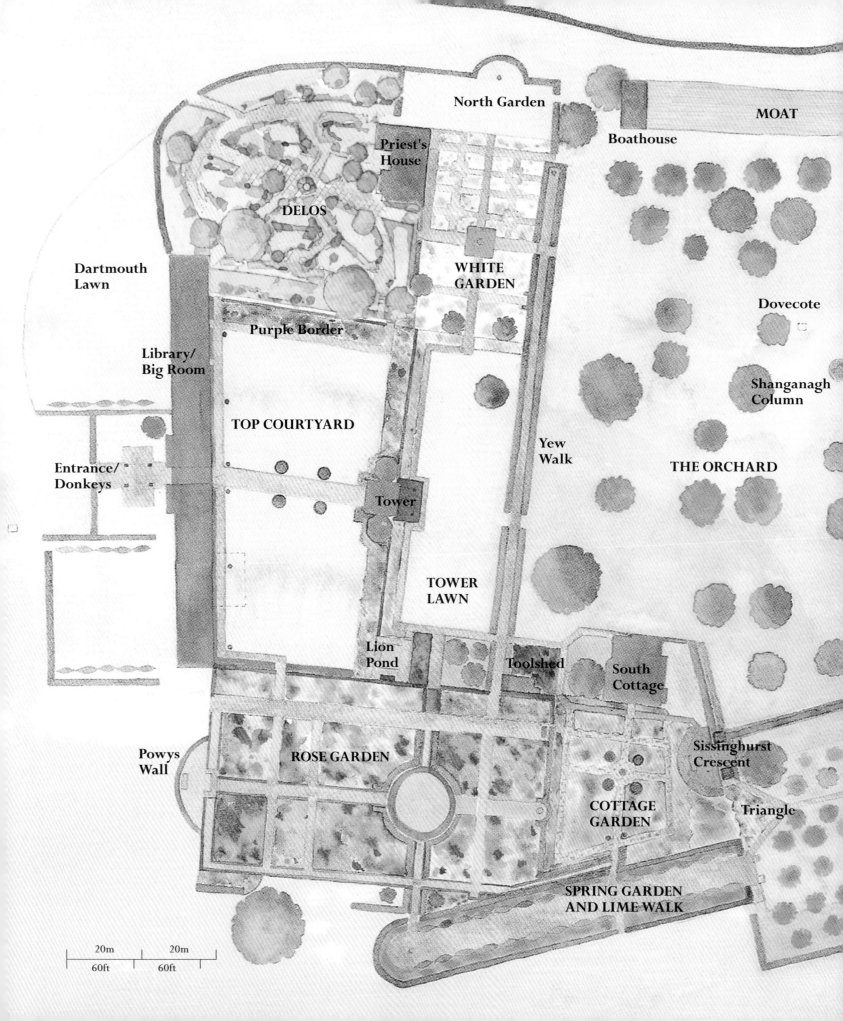

North Garden

MOAT

Boathouse

Priest's House

DELOS

Dartmouth Lawn

WHITE GARDEN

Dovecote

Purple Border

Library/ Big Room

Shanganagh Column

TOP COURTYARD

Yew Walk

THE ORCHARD

Entrance/ Donkeys

Tower

TOWER LAWN

Lion Pond

Toolshed

South Cottage

Powys Wall

ROSE GARDEN

Sissinghurst Crescent

COTTAGE GARDEN

Triangle

SPRING GARDEN AND LIME WALK

20m
60ft

20m
60ft

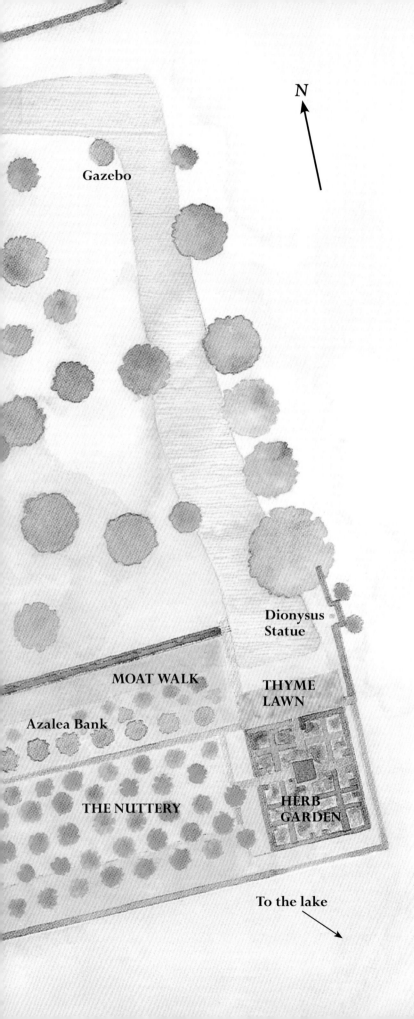

N

Gazebo

Dionysus
Statue

MOAT WALK

THYME
LAWN

Azalea Bank

THE NUTTERY

HERB
GARDEN

To the lake

SISSINGHURST – A TIMELINE

1560s   Sissinghurst House rebuilt on site of medieval manor.

1756–63   Sissinghurst used as gaol during Seven Years War. French prisoners nickname it '*le château*' and it becomes 'Sissinghurst Castle'.

1796   Sissinghurst used as parish workhouse into the early 19th century, when the estate is tenanted out as a farm.

1930   Vita and Harold visit Sissinghurst Castle and purchase it. Cottages cleared from Top Courtyard. Moat Wall unearthed. Nuttery cleared of undergrowth.

1931   Rubbish cleared from whole site. Entrance arch reopened. Lawns laid in Top Courtyard and Tower Lawn. Paths laid in Cottage Garden. Garden by Priest's House planted with roses. Lake excavated.

1932   The family (including teenage sons Ben and Nigel) move in. Path from entrance arch to tower laid and four Irish yews planted. Poplar avenue planted in front meadow. Yew Walk and Rondel planted. Hornbeam hedges planted in Spring Garden. Moat Walk turfed.

1933   Box hedges planted and central path laid in kitchen garden (later Rose Garden). Erechtheum constructed.

1934   Cherry Orchard (later Herb Garden) enclosed by yew hedges. Quartet of yews planted in Cottage Garden.

1935   Powys Wall and north wall of Top Courtyard built.

1936   Limes planted in Lime Walk and paving laid.

1937   Shrub roses planted in Rondel Garden (formerly kitchen garden). Orchard planted as wild garden.

1938   Herb Garden created. Polyanthus carpet established in the Nuttery.

1946   Statue of Dionysus installed.

1948   Thyme Lawn established. The Azalea Bank above Moat Walk planted.

1950   White Garden created.

1959   Pamela Schwerdt and Sibylle Kreutzberger employed as head gardeners.

1962   Vita dies at Sissinghurst, 2 June.

1967   Sienese pots added to Lime Walk and Top Courtyard. Sissinghurst transferred to the National Trust.

1968   Harold dies at Sissinghurst, 1 May. Paving of Rose Garden begun (completed 1969).

1969   Gazebo by Moat constructed. The Herb Garden and Nuttery repaved.

1970   Paving relaid and central arbour added to White Garden.

1971   Wall between Top Courtyard and Rose Garden rebuilt.

1976–77   Lime Walk repaved with York stone and old lime trees replaced.

2003   Boathouse constructed.

2019–20   Delos restored.

I was also at pains to point out that Sissinghurst remained a first-class garden maintained to the highest standards. But these candid observations did ruffle some feathers at the time. As well as going public with my misgivings about the garden, I was arguing from within the Trust for its 're-Vitalization' and also for the appointment of a consultant (Dan Pearson was the suggested candidate) who could assist the head gardener on the overall tone of the garden, as well as its detail, an arrangement that might be extended to other important 'gardens of personality'. Members of the Nicolson family were also – more quietly – urging the Trust to move in the same direction. It is possible that something of the argument registered, as Troy Scott Smith was employed as head gardener in 2013 precisely to 'bring the softness back', as he put it. Shortly thereafter, Dan Pearson was invited to be a 'godparent' of the garden. Sissinghurst has undergone a gradual transformation as a result, with many more roses reintroduced and a more relaxed and romantic style in evidence everywhere. There is good reason to hope that this process will continue under Michelle Cain, who was appointed head gardener in August 2019.

The Nicolson family – notably Vita and Harold's grandchildren Adam and Juliet, and Adam's gardener wife Sarah Raven – have continued to work away in the background, using their influence to reintroduce as much of a sense of authenticity as possible. The family retains the right to occupy the southern part of the front range and the South Cottage for one month a year. This means that, for some of the time, there are still Nicolsons in residence at Sissinghurst. The family's relationship with the Trust has not always been easy, but there is no doubt that they have had an overwhelmingly positive effect on the garden through their knowledge, collective memory and instincts about what is right for the place.

Yet as Adam Nicolson has commented, 'Sissinghurst seems inseparable from anxiety.' There is an underlying feeling that the garden was made by Vita and Harold for themselves alone, and that anyone else – arguably even family members – can therefore be considered as guests only. This intrinsic sense of distance means that it has sometimes proven challenging for people to live happily at Sissinghurst for any length of time. For casual visitors, on the other hand, a feeling of an invasion of someone else's privacy can, in truth, be quite pleasurable.

One of the strengths of the garden is indeed the seriousness of its emotionalism, its occasional air of sweet melancholy. That this was real to Vita is illustrated by her choice of a poem of 1563 by her ancestor Thomas Sackville, for inclusion in the anthology entitled *Another World Than This* (1945), which she edited with Harold. The poem includes the line: 'And sorrowing I to see the summer flowers'. This reflects the truth that the presence of death and decay in gardens is as palpable as life and fecundity, even in the full bloom of summer. It may not apparently be the most uplifting statement to make about a garden, and yet it is possible to draw a strange solace from it. The fleetingness of life, of our existence and that of all living things, is played out in the drama of the garden, where the horror of death and mutability is masked by beauty and the certain knowledge of the continuation of the life cycle. Ultimately, perhaps what is most valuable about our engagement with Sissinghurst is the profound sense of consolation it offers. And for that we should feel a debt of gratitude – to the gardeners, for all the attention and love they have poured into it; to the Nicolson family, who have remained so positively and loyally engaged; and to everyone at the National Trust who has played a role in the garden's survival and presentation to the public over the past half century. Most of all we should feel grateful to its creators, Vita and Harold, who made, as Vita said, 'a garden where none was'. 🐝

RIGHT: The view from the tower towards the Cottage Garden with its quartet of yews, and the toolshed in the foreground by the old castle wall.

CHAPTER ONE

THE APPROACH

'A tired swimmer in the waves of time
I throw my hands up: let the surface close:
Sink down through centuries to another clime,
And buried find the castle and the rose.'

🌹 *Sissinghurst* by Vita Sackville-West, 1931

BOUNDED BY HIGH hedgerows, the lane which runs down towards the little hamlet of Sissinghurst seems to be tunnelling its way through the adjacent fields, where sheep graze beneath old oaks. The castle itself is not visible and there is nothing very remarkable about the views to left and right. If the National Trust sign was not there to direct and reassure us, it is quite possible that we might stop after a few hundred metres to turn around and go back. Surely this farm track is not the way in to a castle?

But it is. After a few more turns under the embowered shade of the old oaks, we find ourselves in the car park, where bird cherries and dog roses form hedges that break up the space, conspiring to create the impression that this is not a car park at a visitor attraction, but a field for cars at a garden that happens to be open to the public that day. Just as it might have been in Vita Sackville-West's and Harold Nicolson's time. They came to live at Sissinghurst in 1932 and opened the garden to the public in 1938, when eight hundred visitors turned up on the first day – an early indication of the hold the place

seems to have over people. The Trust has made efforts in recent years to recreate this informal feel, as if we were all still the 'shillingses', as Vita nicknamed the visiting public. It must be said that it has been quite successful in this regard, against the odds given the numbers involved, with small gaggles of visitors wending their way good-humouredly down the lane towards the castle.

Or is it a farm, after all? That is certainly the first impression of the place, and it is deliberate. The track winds down past a small group of houses and several yards, then the old oast houses which are such a distinctive part of the Wealden landscape, into the large open-sided farmyard beyond. Sissinghurst is a garden of strong shapes on every side – from architecture, from hedges, from plants – and the oasts make for a suitable prelude.

To the right, beyond a big old southern beech (*Nothofagus*), a meadow opens up as the low-slung, warm-brick west (or main) range of the castle itself pops up directly ahead. It is not a moment of pomp and circumstance, this emergence in front of a 'castle' that does look much like a castle – and that is how Vita and Harold liked it. They were well aware that Sissinghurst was, as Harold wrote to his prospective daughter-in-law, 'the strangest conglomeration of shapeless buildings that you ever saw'. On another occasion he described it as

PREVIOUS PAGE: The front range of Sissinghurst Castle seen across the meadow (dominated by yellow rattle). LEFT: The view towards the Elizabethan barn, framed by the southern beech in the meadow.

rattle and especially ox-eye daisy, which is often the way with cultivated meadows. The longer, more uneven sward does away with the assumption, previously, that this was a 'front lawn' beside the house, where families instinctively picnicked and played games.

One rather curious aspect of the meadow is that stretching westwards directly across it is a line of Lombardy poplars. Vita and Harold planted this avenue soon after their arrival, though only one original tree still stands, the others having been grown from cuttings. An avenue is a self-consciously grand feature, and was one of only a few classical estate-scale interventions made by Vita and Harold. At the same time they planted another avenue of thirty-six poplars south-east of the Moat, leading to the Lake, an area that before the war was a particular source of pleasure to Vita.

The old farm pond can be found between the farmhouse and the castle – it had been filled in with rubbish but in the 2010s it was cleared out and restored; in the process, scores of old zinc plant labels were found, and these have been helpful in identifying historical plant varieties. In line with the Trust's subtle ornamentation of the approach to Sissinghurst, the hedge behind the pond has been softened with roses, including 'Splendens' and 'Mannington Mauve Rambler', while a group of crab apples – *Malus* 'Dartmouth', with crimson fruit – stands on the north side of the castle, against Delos. This spot is now known as the Dartmouth Lawn. In Vita's time the whole entrance area was deliberately left more or less unadorned; today's visitor is offered just a little more by way of horticulture. The removal of several mature trees has also opened up views of the surrounding countryside, which were so important to Vita. Sissinghurst should ideally feel as if it is set amid the

a 'ramshackle farm-tumble'. It really would not do to present their house as some kind of 'stately home'; far better to emphasise its qualities of charming dilapidation, and the farm-like setting.

And it is actually, quietly, a rather magical overture. The castle entrance faces slightly uphill across the large expanse of meadow which was, indeed, in former times used for grazing. The old farmer's cottage, a handsome building which these days is the head gardener's house, overlooks the meadow on the far, southern side. The grass is now cut again for hay in late summer, while earlier in the season wildflower plantings give it the appearance of a flowery mead, albeit rather dominated by yellow

*ABOVE LEFT: The tower stands as the epicentre of Sissinghurst; Vita's study and sitting room were on the first floor. ABOVE RIGHT: Foxgloves, hollyhocks (*Alcea pallida*), blue* Campanula lactiflora *and regal lilies growing by the front range, with rose 'Alister Stella Gray' on the wall behind.*

agricultural fields of the Weald, and that sense of interaction is gradually coming back.

The main entrance in the west range is not the only way into the garden. The visitor has the option of walking down to the left, past the end of the west range and Delos, all the way around the outer edge of the Moat, to enter the garden on its south side via either the Nuttery, the Spring Garden and Lime Walk or the Rose Garden. This route creates rather a different perspective and is also less congested. As it is, few people venture beyond the confines of the garden area that is bounded by the Moat and southern fence, though there are several waymarked walks of up to 4.8 kilometres/3 miles around the estate and farmland.

On a sunny day, the brickwork of the main range glows vibrantly orange-red, as if in a process of liquefaction. Even in dull light it can look gorgeously cake-like and spongy. In Vita's time there was only one rose, 'Meg', a climbing hybrid tea, planted against the

wall on this side. A specimen of this variety grows there still, bearing clusters of delicate-looking flowers whose petals become pinker at the edges, their centres a rich apricot orange with red-gold stamens. This colouration could hardly be bettered as a companion to the brickwork, and you can see why Vita felt it sufficient. Today, the other notable rose growing against the wall on either side of the entrance is the highly scented, soft yellow 'Alister Stella Gray', mingling decorously with lower-growing hybrid musk roses 'Cornelia', 'Felicia', 'Penelope' and 'Pink Prosperity', all added in 2015. 'Buff Beauty' has been planted to the left of the entrance, while farther along the range on this side, against the library (known by the family as the Big Room), are yet more climbing and rambling roses, including 'Bleu Magenta' and 'Goldfinch'. Roses have also been planted against the visitor reception ('Wickwar'), on the old dairy ('Phyllis Bide') and on the south ('Blush Rambler') and west ('Mannington Cascade') of the oast houses.

It all makes for a fine prelude. There is even a certain pleasure to be derived from the roses in the chill winter months: an immaculate pruning regime results in its own delicate beauty, with the stems stretched out and pinned in preparation for next season. Pruning has become somewhat more relaxed at Sissinghurst in recent years, leading to plants that are 'craggier and more expressive', as former head gardener Troy Scott Smith put it. It does mean that a specimen can get woodier and larger, but the flowers will be more dispersed and less tightly clustered – redolent of that sense of artless profusion that Vita craved. Two different clematis sing out around the garden entrance at the beginning and end of the season, when 'Meg' is away: first, *Clematis alpina* drapes its abundant purple-blue flowers around the windows; then the little pompom-like purple flowers of *C.* 'Purpurea Plena Elegans' burst through. To the left of the entrance is the elegant *Euphorbia characias* subsp. *wulfenii* 'Lambrook Gold'.

The entrance court was known as 'Donkeys' in Vita's time, and that is how the gardeners still refer to it, though the guidebook does not. The name was inspired by Abdul, a donkey who grazed there and on the meadow. Abdul had been rescued from a pitiable existence in northern Africa in 1934 by Vita, who had him shipped home. He was put to work pulling the mowing machine (before Harold and Vita could stretch to a motor mower), serving as deputy to a leather-booted pony who usually did the job. Abdul was also charged with carrying away weeds in pannier baskets or in a cart. As Vita wrote to Harold of him in 1943: 'He does look so tiny and sweet in his cart, and he is so serious and pulls so hard. I gave him a carrot, but he was too preoccupied to eat it.' Faithful Abdul lived on until 1958 but he is remembered by the name of 'Donkeys'. Animals were always an important part of life at Sissinghurst. Vita had a succession of beloved dogs, including Martin and Rollo the German shepherds, Canute the elkhound and Pippin the cocker spaniel, who

was the mother of Pinka, a gift to Virginia Woolf. The dogs knew it was time for a walk when they heard the crack of their mistress's fountain-pen lid being put back on. Vita even wrote the text for a book of photographs entitled *Faces: Profiles of Dogs* (1961), which includes descriptions of forty-four breeds (Corgi: 'docile minion', Afghan hound: 'like somebody's elderly Aunt Lavinia, who nourishes a secret passion for the Vicar', and so on). There were doves in the Orchard dovecote, ducks and water-fowl on the Moat and, of course, the sight, smell and sound of livestock all around.

Today, the entrance forecourt is a rather smart and formal overture. A pair of little lawns edged with box flanks the path, where the wooden ticketing kiosk stands. A short run of lime pleach stands on each side of this bijou forecourt. The fine bronze Bagatelle urns here are four out of six survivors from an original set of eight that were a gift from Lady Sackville, Vita's mother (the other pair is on the tower steps overlooking the Tower Lawn). They are typically planted up with the vivid pink but rather dapper *Verbena* (now *Glandularia*) 'Sissinghurst', though the planting is refreshed throughout the year (snowdrops in winter).

And then the visitor gains a first proper glimpse of the tower directly ahead, framed by Sissinghurst's gateway. It is a transfixing moment, especially as the tower has not loomed particularly large until now. There is generally an introductory film showing in a room to the right of the entrance – but many visitors will be drawn inexorably towards the castle's precincts: the inner sanctum. 🦋

RIGHT: The avenue of poplars traversing the meadow was an early intervention made by Harold and Vita, in 1932.

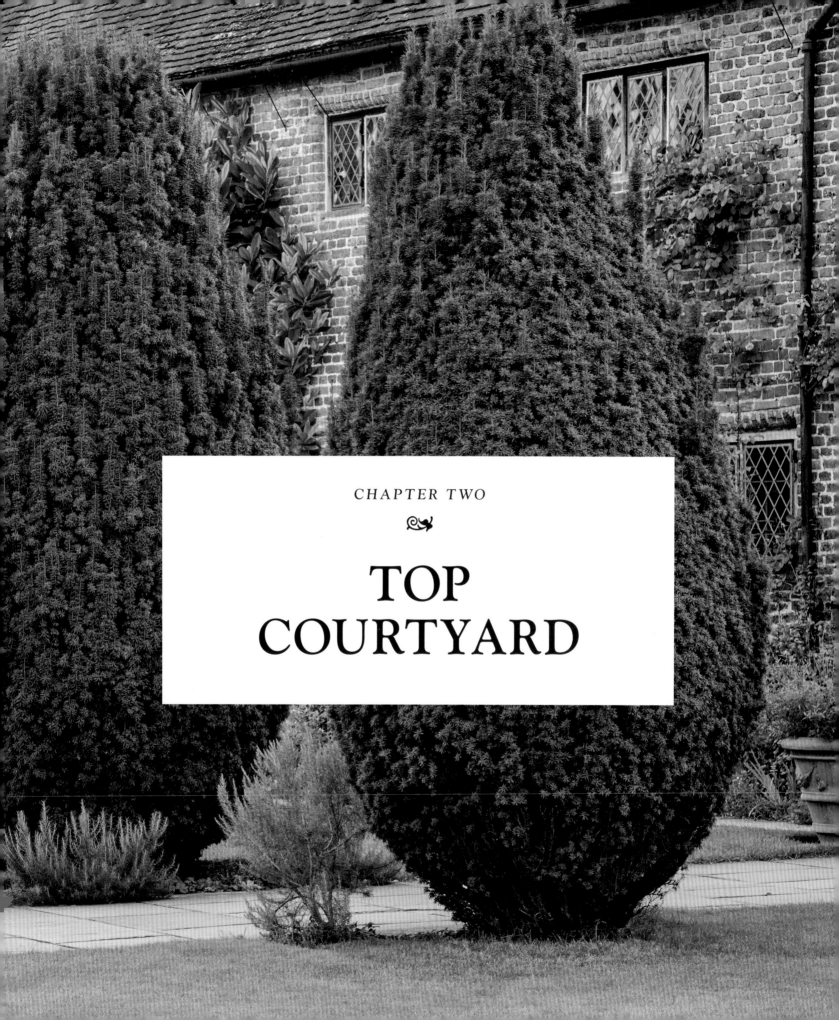

CHAPTER TWO

TOP COURTYARD

'Sissinghurst has a quality of mellowness, of retirement, of unflaunting dignity, which is just what we wanted to achieve…I think it is mainly due to the succession of privacies: the forecourt, the first arch, the main court, the tower arch, the lawn, the orchard. All a series of escapes from the world, giving the impression of cumulative escape.'

Letter from Harold Nicolson to Vita Sackville-West, 26 October 1948

THE TOP COURTYARD is the entrance hall to the garden – for Sissinghurst functions first of all as a garden, not as a house or dwelling place. There is little sense of ceremony as you enter the courtyard on the level (no steps down from the entrance lodge, as Vita insisted) but this space is undoubtedly imposing, with the turreted tower ahead and the four Irish yews lining the flagged central path, standing to attention like two pairs of portly yeomen of the guard. Yet it is not unwelcoming in any way. The tower is more romantic than anything – less a fortified keep than an enchanting escape. The curious little capped roofs to the turrets, which seem more quaintly French-Norman than English, enhance the domestic air.

The first thing that strikes the visitor is the breadth of the courtyard, which stretches almost the length of the west range and is considerably wider than it is deep. It creates a feeling not so much that you are in a 'room' – which is the great cliché concerning Sissinghurst – but that you have now crossed the threshold of a special place,

PREVIOUS PAGE: The yew topiaries are left to grow large and somewhat misshapen, adding to the character of the courtyard. LEFT: The view of the tower from the Purple Border, with dahlias 'Requiem' and 'Pink Michigan'.

and that choices will have to be made. You are all too aware that this garden was created as a private space, and that accordingly it harbours its secrets.

Light plays an important role in the courtyard: the topiaries and the buildings cast strong shadows, while the planes of the lawns and walls seem to catch the light and the moment, absorbing and then reflecting the kind of day it is. It is hard to believe that, when Vita and Harold arrived, the entrance arch was bricked up and there were some motley cobbled-together cottages leaning against the western wall.

As it transpires, the Top Courtyard proves to be a deliberately understated prelude to a series of intensely expressive garden spaces. The idea of a garden space as a room was neither new nor Vita and Harold's invention, as is sometimes supposed. Gardens of successive enclosures were well-established in late-Victorian and Edwardian England and in their own time numerous 'gardens of rooms' had already been made, not least at Hidcote, Rodmarton and Iford Manor. What was novel about Sissinghurst was the composition of the rooms, and the way they were chiefly dependent on horticultural, as opposed to architectural, effects. Mainstream Arts and Crafts style was notably architectural in outlook, its

leading protagonists being architects rather than gardeners (the Jekyll and Lutyens partnership the exception that proved the rule). There were professional planting designers, such as Norah Lindsay, but only William Robinson of Gravetye Manor showed the way as a garden-maker who was as interested in horticulture as architecture. As the garden's style-setter, Vita duly looked to Robinson above all as her guide and mentor.

The Top Courtyard is the most castle-like space at Sissinghurst, for the main surviving fragments are all strongly present here: the tower, the west range and several walls. When Harold and Vita got to Sissinghurst they found the 'castle' consisted of just this one range that was more or less intact, with three odd, stand-alone buildings behind it: two cottages and the great old tower itself. Without that proud edifice standing defiantly at the centre, the place would have seemed an unprepossessing wreck. In addition, there was the remnant of a moat along part of the eastern and northern perimeter, and various bits of old wall — elements that proved crucial in the making of the garden and lend it much of its atmosphere today. Sissinghurst was never a real castle, anyhow: it was the French prisoners of war incarcerated here in the 18th century who had ironically dubbed it *le château* — and the name stuck. Vita and Harold's first and greatest stroke of genius at Sissinghurst lay in their decision to take it on at all — seeing the potential for a garden at this pseudo-castle set in the midst of a rubbish dump, then embracing all the work that lay in store and, in the process, spending most of their available funds on the project.

A pair of massive terracotta pots is positioned just inside the court beyond the gateway, and there are four

ABOVE LEFT: Aeoniums and nerines in pots decorate the entrance arch. BELOW LEFT: Each day the gardeners lay out a display of notable blooms in the garden. RIGHT: Yellow verbascum and rose 'Meg' on the east-facing wall of the Top Courtyard.

more pots ranged along this western side. (These were picked up by Nigel Nicolson at a nursery near Siena.) This sextet in the Top Courtyard is always planted identically, with orlaya and *Iris* 'Perry's Blue' in spring, perhaps followed by a combination of *Cerinthe major* 'Purpurascens' with *Salvia* 'Nachtvlinder', erigeron and lavender. In Vita's time there were also large rosemary bushes around the flanks of the gateway.

While the overall initial impression is of order and austerity, if the visitor turns around they will find a pleasing jumble of horticultural-architectural effects against this inner side of the west range. The stone troughs and sinks along the building were fished out of Sissinghurst's outbuildings by Vita soon after her arrival. 'I like the habit of pot gardening,' she remarked. 'It reminds me of the South – Italy, Spain, Provence, where pots of carnations and zinnias are stood carelessly about.' Vita's troughs, of course, had to have some kind of pedigree of their own, and in her *New Statesman*

column in the late 1930s she claimed: 'I myself possess a trough which I found lying in a pig-sty, and which I discovered was traditionally known as Wat Tyler's foot-bath…It is now filled with small bright blue flowers – gentians, lithospermum, and *Omphalodes luciliae*.' Today, these are regularly renewed in experimental spirit with, for example, alpines or violets in spring, then tulips, through subjects such as *Gazania* 'Freddie', nemesia and *Euphorbia myrsinites*, and dahlias in late summer.

The flagged path along this western perimeter of the courtyard is narrow, so the impression is of tiptoeing around the edge of the space. The bed against the building is also narrow, and the section south (turning right) of the entrance arch is packed with interesting subjects, from a range of violets in spring (*Viola* 'Bowles's Black', *V. cornuta*, *V. labradorica*) to irises ('Benton Evora', 'Banbury Beauty') and dianthus (*Dianthus chinensis* and *D. knappii* 'Yellow Harmony'). Choice shrubs have been selected for later in the season, including *Ceanothus*

'Tuxedo' and *Euphorbia mellifera*, along with climbers, such as purple-flowered *Solanum crispum*. And a giant *Magnolia grandiflora* stands proud in the middle of it all, its glossy foliage making its presence felt at all times of the year, and its flowers like 'great white pigeons settling among dark leaves', as Vita put it. The all-season theme continues in the section to the north of the entrance arch, with several more ceanothus ('Percy Picton' and 'Puget Blue'), erysimums, hardy geraniums such as 'Ballerina', hebes, *Tulbaghia violacea*, and roses, including the pink and intensely scented rambler 'Albertine' and 'Cardinal de Richelieu', enrobed in rich purple petals. Irises are a feature in spring (*Iris pumila*, *I. tuberosa*, *I. graminea* and *I.* 'Green Spot') with tulips (*Tulipa* 'Bronze Charm', *T. saxatilis*, *T. tarda*) following on later in the season.

The entire northern side of the Top Courtyard, against a wall Vita and Harold had built in 1935, is given over to a purple perennial border. This was conceived by Vita as a rich velveteen tapestry made up of the decadent, somehow aristocratic, colours she loved most, many of them more blue than purple, as she was to observe in her column in the *Observer*. In Vita's time it was a profusion of rich purple and pink shades from campanulas, wallflowers, hardy geraniums, pansies, aquilegias, delphiniums, penstemons, liatris, dahlias, iris, asters and alliums, with vines, clematis and smoke bush (*Cotinus*) behind – all offset by scarlet *Rosa moyesii*. A moodily intriguing sort of confection.

The Purple Border is the first real indication visitors gain that, when it comes to planting, this is going to be a different kind of garden. For Sissinghurst did not turn out to be in any way 'quintessentially English' – as it is sometimes described. How could it be entirely English,

ABOVE LEFT: Penstemon *'Andenken an Friedrich Hahn' and* Catananche caerulea, *backed by artemisia – growing by the tower. ABOVE RIGHT: A late-summer scene in the south-east corner:* Dahlia *'Requiem' with* Symphyotrichum novae-angliae *'Lye End Beauty' and* Aster x frikartii.

when Vita's own veins coursed with Spanish Gypsy blood? Her maternal grandmother, Pepita, was a Spanish dancer and famed beauty about whom Vita wrote an entire book.

One of the things that attracted Vita to Sissinghurst in the first place was its hint of foreignness, as she indicated in her article in the RHS *Journal* in 1953:

> It was a romantic place and, within the austerity of Harold Nicolson's straight lines, must be romantically treated. Very English, very Kentish, with its distant prospect over woods and cornfields and hop-gardens and the North Downs, and the pointed oast-houses and the great barn, it yet had something foreign about it: a Norman manor-house perhaps; a faint echo of something slightly more southern, something that belonged to the Contes de Perrault.

(Charles Perrault published a celebrated collection of fairy tales in 1697, several later retold by the Brothers Grimm.) It seems that a tension lies at the heart of the garden's very fabric, just as there was within Vita herself. Sissinghurst was never going to be a well-mannered garden exhibiting taste and decorum, in the Edwardian manner. For Vita, it was to present itself, superficially, as the apogee of English romanticism expressed in the form of a garden (that never-ending saturnalia of natural history) – yet it would never sink to complacency in its Englishness, containing within it transgressive intimations of the 'foreign' and the 'exotic'. For Harold, it would be a theatre in which moments of high drama and subtle decadence could be staged. For both, it was above all an emotional, sensual and hedonistic experience.

Another impetus for the creation of a rather exotic-looking garden – as a declaration of intent at the very

LEFT: The mauve theme extends across the beds of the Top Courtyard: (top left) Dianthus carthusianorum; (top right) Phlox paniculata; (bottom left) Salvia nemorosa 'Caradonna'; and (middle right) Clematis 'Perle d'Azur', with white notes from (middle) Orlaya grandiflora and (bottom right) Campanula lactiflora 'Assendon Pearl', with onopordum beyond.

start of Sissinghurst – was Vita and Harold's romantic attachment to the Middle East. They had spent the first year of their married life together in Constantinople and went on to travel across Morocco, Algeria and other parts of North Africa, while Harold was posted to Tehran for several years in the mid 1920s. Vita recalled the first garden they had made, in Constantinople, in the poem 'Dhji-Han-Ghir', dedicated to Harold, in a volume entitled *Poems of West and East* (1917):

> For years it had been neglected,
> This wilderness garden of ours...
>
> ...And the fruit-trees grew in profusion,
> Quince and pomegranate and vine,
> And the roses in rich confusion
> With the lilac intertwine

The memory stayed with them, and Vita's first dream of Sissinghurst was just such a vision of fruiting trees and shrubs tumbling over old walls among the roses. Despite her love of the Kentish Weald, Vita wanted to transcend the local geography, transporting us to other places by horticultural means. She visited Harold in Persia twice and they travelled across the desert to Isfahan, botanising in the hills and finding the small species tulips and gladioli which she envisaged in the Nuttery and on the Thyme Lawn. The pink damask rose 'Ispahan', still grown at Sissinghurst (in the Rose Garden), was part of this Persian legacy, along with *Rosa foetida* and *Tulipa sylvestris* (both found in the Cottage Garden). Vita and Harold never shied away from including plants and artefacts from other parts of the world – there is the low bowl on lion feet in the Herb Garden, for example, while the Vestal Virgin statue shaded by the silver-grey foliage of a pear tree adds a soupçon of something distinctively un-English to the White Garden. The Dutch still-life paintings from Vita's Knole childhood presumably

also had an influence (she hung several of them in her bedroom) with their burgeoning blossoms seemingly overflowing the canvas. The instinct, at Sissinghurst, is always towards ornamentation and enrichment. All the lilies are to be gilded. This is a garden of baroque effects. There is also something Eastern, perhaps, about Harold's layout: the sense of successive enclosures, long corridor-like effects, the cruciform paths, the sensuous privacies.

In October 2018 the entire Purple Border was replanted, which meant that almost everything was taken out except for one original *Rosa moyesii*. This was a plant particularly valued by Vita, and her description of it is so extraordinary, and so encapsulates her style, it demands to be repeated:

> *This is a Chinese rose and looks it. If ever a plant reflected all that we had ever felt about the delicacy, lyricism, and design of a Chinese drawing,* Rosa moyesii *is that plant…'Go, lovely rose'. She goes indeed, and quickly. Three weeks at most sees her through her yearly explosion of beauty. But her beauty is such that she must be grown for the sake of those three weeks in June. During that time her branches will tumble with the large, single rose-red flower of her being. It is of an indescribable colour. I hold a flower of it here in my hand now, and find myself defeated in description. It is like the colour I imagine Petra to be, if one caught it at just the right moment of sunset. It is like some colours in a rug from Isfahan. It is like the dyed leather sheaf of an Arab knife.*

Now, vines and clematis such as 'Perle d'Azur' and 'Étoile Violette' again clothe the back wall, next to quince, damson and nectarine trees, added in recognition of Vita's original emphasis on fruit. Here are masses of *Campanula* 'Sarastro', *Salvia nemorosa* 'Amethyst' and 'Caradonna', *Lythrum virgatum* 'Dropmore Purple', *Phlox divaricata* 'Clouds of Perfume' and *P.* x *arendsii* 'Luc's Lilac', *Sidalcea* 'Purpetta', *Dianthus carthusianorum*, *Vernonia arkansana*, *Verbascum phoeniceum* 'Violetta', *Symphyotrichum turbinellum* and *Achillea millefolium* 'Lilac Beauty'. They offset groups of delphiniums, penstemons, lilacs, lupins, malvas and specimens such as *Calycanthus* 'Aphrodite'. The whole effect is perhaps lighter and less congested than it was previously, despite the profusion. There are also 'old-fashioned' veronicas and sweet Williams lower down, with hyacinths and tulips there for the spring, mingling with wallflowers. Irises are a feature earlier in the season – 'Blue Boy', 'Savoir Faire' and, of course, 'Sissinghurst' among them – while late-season interest is provided by asters, such as *Aster* x *frikartii* 'Wunder von Stäfa', *Symphyotrichum novi-belgii* 'Audrey', *S. novae-angliae* 'Lye End Beauty' and dahlias including 'Edinburgh' and 'Requiem'. The number of asters across the whole garden has been reduced, and this (and the Spring Garden) is

*OPPOSITE: Tulips including 'Showcase', 'Bleu Aimable' and 'Black Hero' bubble away in the Purple Border in spring, with wisteria coming on the east wall and perennial honesty (*Lunaria rediviva*) below. ABOVE: The exotic damask rose 'Ispahan' reminded Vita of her travels in the Middle East.*

'Empire Blue', *Tradescantia* 'Purewell Giant' and masses of geraniums. The border to the right (south) includes *Cercis siliquastrum* 'Bodnant', hostas, salvias, *Thalictrum delavayi* and roses 'Cardinal de Richelieu', purple-pink 'William Lobb' and 'Albertine'. A range of clematis adorn the back wall. Certain contemporary perennial plants – veronicastrum, sanguisorba and eupatorium, for example – have been added to the borders here, but they do not look anachronistically fashionable in this historic garden because they are planted singly in the midst of the borders rather than in drifts towards the back, in the 21st-century manner.

With the south border of the Top Courtyard, the intention is to create the impression of a wave or surge of plants flowing up and over the garden, perhaps metaphorically crashing into the Rose Garden beyond. There are rambler roses on the walls – purple 'Veilchenblau' and pink 'May Queen' on the left – and in front an exuberant mass of lupins, foxgloves, fennel, centranthus, silene, digitalis, red campion and rosebay willhowherb. Specimens of *Hydrangea anomala* subsp. *petiolaris* help lend structure to the border.

In Vita's time the south-west corner of this courtyard was devoted to aquilegias, or columbines as she would have called them, and many hundreds self-seeded in the garden, but problems with mildew has meant they are now dying out at Sissinghurst. The area is being revamped, with the mainstay remaining a 'Kew Rambler' rose (pink flowers fading to white, with profuse orange hips) and the white *Camellia japonica* 'Alba Simplex'.

Now, a delightfully small doorway in the wall beckons the visitor on towards the Rose Garden: the glory of Sissinghurst. 🦋

their main showing in the garden today. The intended feel of the Purple Border is for a soft, mingled effect, as opposed to the strong contrasts in foliage, form and colour that were preferred by Gertrude Jekyll and which came into vogue again in the 1990s, and perhaps became the expectation of visitors at that time. There are several roses here, too: on the right, 'Paul Transom', 'Spectabilis' and 'Meg', the last complemented by indigofera and shiny leaves of myrtle, which Vita had in her wedding posy.

The borders on the east of the court are more difficult; they must act as buttresses on each side of the tower and accordingly contain larger perennials and shrubs so that a sense of scale is maintained. In addition, the plants must be tough enough to cope with the down-draughts created by the presence of the tower; this is one of the coldest parts of the garden. The section on the left (north) side of the tower features such sturdy performers as *Buddleja davidii*

ABOVE: Narcissi in one of the stone troughs set against the west range; most of these containers were discovered littered around the site. RIGHT: Tulips 'Negrita', 'Ronaldo' and 'Havran' in giant Sienese terracotta pots, with Ceanothus 'Puget Blue' blooming on the wall behind.

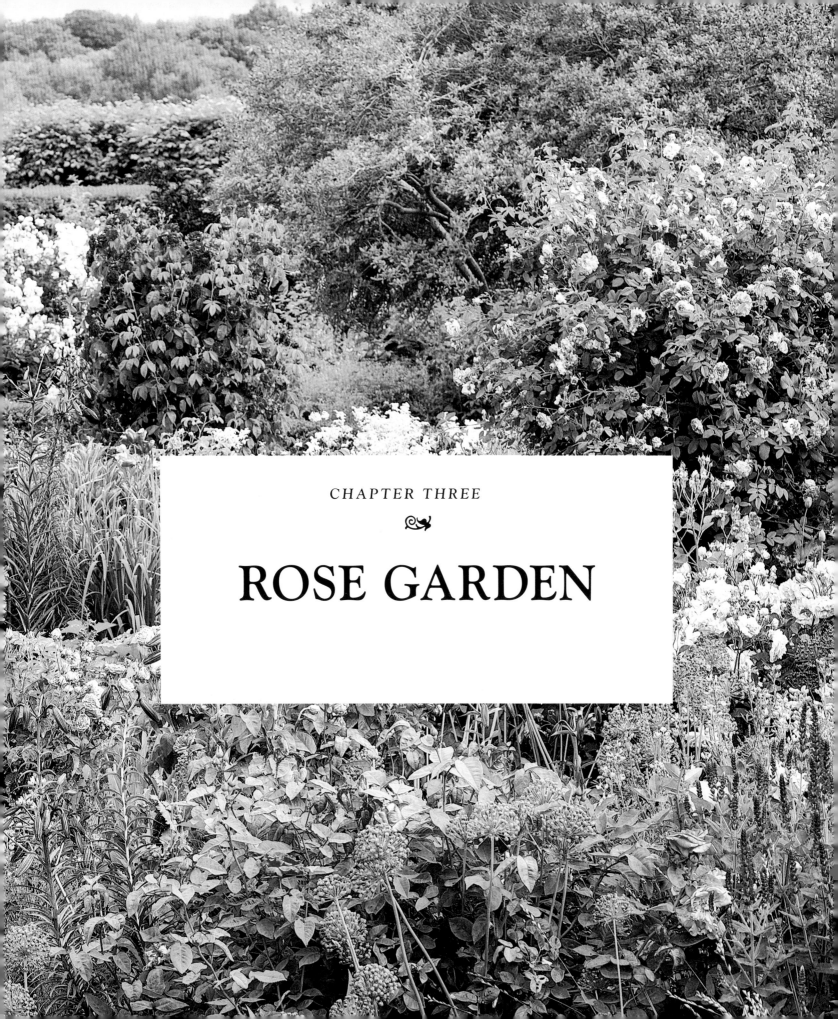

CHAPTER THREE

ROSE GARDEN

CLIMBER
'ALBERTINE'

'And the fruit-trees grew in profusion,
Quince and pomegranate and vine,
And the roses in rich confusion
With the lilac intertwine'

🌹 'Dhji-Han-Ghir' by Vita Sackville-West, 1917

ROSES ARE THE very essence of Sissinghurst. There are around six hundred dispersed across the garden, climbing on those characterful brick walls or 'foaming in an unorthodox way in the midst of flower borders', as Vita put it. In the Rose Garden itself, the idea was that roses should come at you from all sides – thrusting up from planting beds, meandering across the crumbling brick walls, appearing suddenly at indecisive corners. It is the roses, above all, which create that feeling of transcendency and escape at Sissinghurst, a sensation that visitors cherish to the point of addiction.

It was a rose that was the only identifiable flower that Vita and Harold found when they first visited the place in April 1930: an old-fashioned gallica, which they dubbed 'Sissinghurst Castle', was growing in an unregarded corner of the neglected Orchard. It must have seemed to them like an omen, of sorts. In her diary Vita noted simply of Sissinghurst: 'Fell flat in love with it.' From that moment, the garden's fate was set: Sissinghurst

was to be a rose garden above all. But these would not be any roses. It would be a garden chiefly of 'old roses', of the sort that a select group of horticultural connoisseurs were beginning to appreciate over and above the rather gaudy and too-perfect modern hybrid teas which were thought, somewhat snobbishly, to be the preserve of suburban gardens and 'rose fanciers' who grew for show (though Vita herself had, in fact, grown many hybrid teas, such as apricot 'Lady Hillingdon', at her previous home, Long Barn). Famously, the first thing Vita did at Sissinghurst, even before they had signed the deeds of ownership, was to plant a rose, 'Madame Alfred Carrière', on the south wall of South Cottage. It grows there still.

Vita was always interested in roses – not excluding the 'wild' or species roses. Such plants have an unpretentious and frankly unruly hedgerow air which she cherished. As her poetic near-contemporary Rupert Brooke wrote:

Unkempt about those hedges blows
An English unofficial rose

Vita liked what was unofficial. As she once commented: 'English people do not like being organised; they like

PREVIOUS PAGE: The apparently artless romanticism of the Rose Garden must be carefully managed. LEFT: The sight of roses growing on warm brick walls is one of the abiding pleasures of Sissinghurst. Here, Rosa 'Albertine' clambers above a cluster of marguerite daisies.

to live their own lives as best seems to them.' It is a libertarian creed which sits deep inside many English people, transcending political boundaries. Traditional, apparently artless cottage-garden style is its horticultural corollary. Vita wanted Sissinghurst to seem always poised just on the edge of anarchy, as if it was a once-beautiful garden abandoned to its fate. (It is no surprise that Sissinghurst has often been identified as an embodiment of Frances Hodgson Burnett's *The Secret Garden* of 1911, which was still a cult book at the time Vita and Harold moved in.) And, despite its intermittent frissons of 'exoticism', Sissinghurst was to be an English garden. This was real and urgent to Vita who, with her Spanish Gypsy grandmother, could never identify as wholly English, and was therefore at times almost desperate to assert her Englishness and, within that, her Kentishness.

Vita's interest in roses was piqued afresh by a book, Edward Bunyard's *Old Garden Roses*, which appeared in 1936. Bunyard, a Kentish nurseryman, was one of the greatest plant connoisseurs and the very doyen among discerning voices on the topic of fruit grown for flavour. His book on old roses reflected an obsession with near-vanished varieties which clung on only in the gardens of a few knowledgeable gardeners of romantic disposition in Britain, northern France and Belgium. In the late 1930s Vita began buying — direct from Bunyard, who would come for lunch — and growing the roses he recommended, and also descending upon the gardens of other old-rose connoisseurs, who then numbered in their tens rather than hundreds. The innovative floral arranger Constance Spry was a keen grower of old roses, as was Lawrence Johnston at Hidcote, Mrs Leonard Messel at Nymans, Bobby James at St Nicholas, nurserywoman Hilda Murrell and Nancy Lindsay, daughter of the planting designer Norah Lindsay. All of them were special gardening friends of Vita's and some, notably Spry, provided advice on the garden's design. Johnston's garden, Hidcote, proved inspirational in terms of horticultural tone, with Vita looking back

and commenting in 1949: 'It resembles a cottage garden, or rather, a series of cottage gardens, in so far as the plants grow in a jumble, flowering shrubs mingle with roses, herbaceous plants with bulbous subjects, climbers scrambling over hedges, seedlings coming up wherever they have chosen to show themselves.' This could equally be a description of her Sissinghurst.

The nurseryman Graham Stuart Thomas, later chief gardens adviser at the National Trust, joined the group after a short while (with his colleague James Russell) and eventually produced a book entitled *The Old Shrub Roses* (1956), which eclipses even Bunyard's in terms of information, though it lacks its charm. These supplicants at the altar of the old shrub roses swapped plants or made each other gifts of them, used them in the house for table decorations or left them to take over their gardens.

Vita was instinctively a historian, with a strong romantic bent. She had a tendency to immerse herself in a period so that she seemed to dwell more in that moment of the past than in the present. This extended to her understanding of flowers. She was acutely aware of the traditional value placed on the rose in both garden and house in England, as well as its identification with the female sex. The rose was the mainstay of the medieval Mary garden, an enclosed space dedicated to the Virgin and made close to the house, traditionally the preserve of the women of the household, who could read or sew in this fragrant bower. The rose meant more to Vita than simply its beauty; it was a symbol of the continuity of English country life in its finer aspects, and an emblem of English womanhood.

The old roses had fallen from favour chiefly because they flower just once in a season, for a glorious month or so, and then they are gone — unlike the hybrid teas and

RIGHT: Old-rose heaven: pale pink hybrid musk 'Felicia' in the middle, with 'William Shakespeare' behind and lighter pink 'Vanity' just beyond. Farther back, on a frame near the door, is the purple-blue 'Tour de Malakoff'.

other modern roses, which can go on and on. The most popular post-war rose, aptly named 'Peace', was a case in point: a large-petalled hybrid tea with pale yellow flowers tinged with crimson. For Vita and her confederates, a show-off rose such as this was frankly vulgar when placed next to an old damask, gallica or centifolia, with their shyly chaotic bundles of flower clusters, often in subtler pinks and whites, or else in satisfyingly pure, rich and deep colours. As Vita explained in a lecture given at the RHS in 1961:

> You will not find amongst the old roses, the brilliant red and orange and cherry of many modern varieties. They tend to be more sombre — I had almost said more medieval — less frivolous, less gay. To me, they recall the brocades of ecclesiastical vestments, the glow of mosaics, the texture of Oriental carpets.

The flowers of old shrub roses are neither 'repeat' nor 'perpetual' nor 'disease-resistant', which is what the nurseries thought people wanted, while the blooms are smaller than the modern hybrids, though more profuse in their one gigantic rush of flowering. Ultimately, the old shrub roses are possessed of certain characteristics that romantically inclined gardeners such as Vita cherish above all else: personality, poise, charm, modesty.

There is texture, as well — a quality sometimes forgotten in discussions of flowers. As Vita put it in one of her columns in 1950: 'I could go on for ever, but always I should come back to the idea of embroidery and of velvet and of the damask with which some of them share their name.' Vita thought of colour in three dimensions: colour, form and scent, with texture bound up in all three. She understood that the surface quality

RIGHT: The roses 'Comte de Chambord' (front) 'Felicia' (middle) and 'Constance Spry' (upper right) are supported by plants such as purple Salvia nemorosa, *allium seed heads and the leaves of irises.*

KEY VARIETIES IN THE ROSE GARDEN

AB 'Alain Blanchard'; **AD** 'Alfred de Dalmas'; **AM** 'Rose d'Amour'; **AO** 'Adélaïde d'Orléans'; **BB** 'Buff Beauty'; **BC** 'Belle de Crécy'; **BD** 'Blush Damask'; **BDC** 'Blanche Double de Coubert'; **BG** 'Baron Girod de l'Ain'; **BM** 'Blanche Moreau'; **C** 'Céleste'; **CB** 'Cécile Brünner'; **CC** *R. × centifolia* 'Cristata'; **CDC** 'Comte de Chambord'; **CEL** 'Célina'; **CH** 'Coupe d'Hébé'; **CJ** 'Claire Jacquier'; **CM** 'Charles de Mills'; **CO** 'Conditorum'; **CR** 'Cardinal de Richelieu'; **CS** 'Constance Spry'; **D** 'Debutante'; **DA** 'Duchesse d'Angoulême'; **DG** 'Duc de Guiche'; **DM** 'Duchesse de Montebello'; **DN** 'Danaë'; **DPF** 'Deuil de Paul Fontaine'; **DU** 'Dunwich Rose'; **E** 'Eglantyne'; **EH** 'Étoile de Hollande'; **F** 'Felicia'; **FL** 'Fantin-Latour'; **FP** 'Félicité Perpétue'; **FPA** 'Félicité Parmentier'; **FPI** 'Ferdinand Pichard'; **G** 'The Garland'; **GA** 'Gruss an Aachen'; **GK** 'Général Kléber'; **GW** 'Great Western'; **HB** 'Honorine de Brabant'; **HM** 'Henri Martin'; **I** 'Ispahan'; **IJ** 'Impératrice Joséphine'; **K** 'Kathleen'; **KG** 'Königin von Dänemark'; **KH** 'Kathleen Harrop'; **KM** 'Kordes' Magenta'; **KR** 'Kew Rambler'; **L14** 'Louis XIV'; **L** 'Lanei'; **LE** 'Leda'; **LC** 'Lilac Charm'; **LL** 'Lavender Lassie'; **MEC** 'Mme. Ernest Calvat'; **MH** 'Mme. Hardy'; **MIP** 'Mme. Isaac Péreire'; **MLB** 'Mme. Lauriol de Barny'; **MOF** 'Mrs Oakley Fisher';

MP 'Mme. Plantier'; **MQ** 'May Queen'; **MQS** *R. spinosissima* 'Mary, Queen of Scots'; **N** 'Nestor'; **NC** 'Noisette Carnée'; **NM** 'Nur Mahal'; **NY** 'Nuits de Young'; **P** 'Penelope'; **PE** 'Purple East'; **PLP** 'Paul's Lemon Pillar'; **PN** 'Paul Neyron'; **PR** 'Paul Ricault'; **PS** 'Président de Sèze'; **PX** 'Pax'; **RAM** *R. × alba* 'Alba Maxima'; **RD** 'Rêve d'Or'; **RDV** 'Reine des Violettes'; **RG** *R. glauca*; **RGO** *R. gallica* var. *officinalis*; **RGV** *R. gallica* 'Versicolor' (rosa mundi); **RH** 'Roseraie de l'Hay'; **RMV** 'Rose-Marie Viaud'; **RN** *R. nitida*; **ROV** *R. × odorata* 'Viridiflora'; **RR** 'Rose du Roi à Fleurs Pourpres'; **RS** 'Spectabilis'; **RV** 'Reine Victoria'; **RW** *R. willmottiae*; **S** 'Salet'; **SC** 'Sissinghurst Castle'; **SDJ** 'Souvenir du Docteur Jamain'; **SM** 'Souvenir de la Malmaison'; **SP** 'Stanwell Perpetual'; **SSC** *R. spinosissima* 'Single Cherry'; **SVF** 'Sarah van Fleet'; **SWM** *R. × centifolia* 'Shailer's White Moss'; **T** 'Thelma'; **TS** 'Tuscany Superb'; **UBF** 'Ulrich Brünner Fils'; **UP** *R. × centifolia* 'Unique Panachée'; **V** 'Vanity'; **VB** 'Variegata di Bologna'; **VBR** 'La Ville de Bruxelles'; **VI** *R. villosa*; **W3** *R. spinosissima* 'William III'; **WD** 'Duplex' (Wolley-Dod's rose); **WDY** *R. × harisonii* 'Williams' Double Yellow'; **WL** 'William Lobb'; **WS** 'William Shakespeare'; **WW** 'White Wings'; **Z** 'Ziegeunerknabe'; **ZD** 'Zéphirine Drouhin'

of petals, or leaves, or the way rain or dew is held on them, has an effect on underlying colouration, and that sensations of texture can be associated with scent as well.

The Rose Garden started life in 1932 as the vegetable garden. Five years later, at around the time that Bunyard's book appeared, Vita and Harold decided to turn it over to roses. The yew Rondel at its centre had been made to distract from the fact that the space is neither a perfect square nor rectangle (in Vita's time it was, in fact, known as the Rondel Garden). The layout appears rigorously geometric, a fearful symmetry to frame the gorgeous scented chaos of the flowers themselves. As Vita reminds us in her foreword to Graham Thomas's book, roses are not just flowers but shrubs, first and foremost, and to that end the beds in the Rose Garden were made large enough to contain a number of specimens crammed together. This was Vita's mantra, of course: 'cram, cram, cram every chink and cranny' – though the context of this passage tends to be overlooked. She did not mean that you should cram every flower bed with plants, though in practice that is what she did. Vita hated mealy-mouthed, mean-minded English paucity, especially given the years of wartime austerity everyone had lived through. She wanted her cup to be full to overflowing. For Vita, it was worth spending your last penny on something beautiful rather than something useful. 'I like generosity wherever I find it, whether in gardens or elsewhere,' she wrote. 'I hate to see things scrimp and scrubby.'

ABOVE: From the tower, the yew Rondel – a feature indebted to Hidcote – is perhaps the most prominent architectural moment in the garden layout.

The Rondel effectively cuts the garden in half, with an upper rose garden to the west – where the real action is – and a lower rose garden to the east. In addition, there is the brick-walled apsidal platform at the west end, which was introduced by Harold as a raised vantage point and a moment of respite from the horticultural effusiveness all around. (A classic, Lutyens-designed bench is placed there, a gift from Lady Sackville, who had had a liaison with the designer.) It also screens off the cutting garden, greenhouses and other 'business' areas over the wall. Today, the curving Powys Wall, as it is known, after Albert Powys, the architect Vita and Harold used, is adorned by the clematis 'Perle d'Azur', and clothed with *Vitis vinifera* and *Parthenocissus henryana*. (The clematis is these days a famed Sissinghurst plant, but it was added after Vita's time by the National Trust.) The effectiveness of this platform divides opinion. (Vita, for one, hated it.) Too large and rather bald in its dimensions, the dais and brick wall sit rather awkwardly in the space. It is one of very few designed features here which appear to come from the standard vocabulary of the Arts and Crafts garden, when the great strength of this garden's design as a whole is its non-standard originality, boldness and verve. The same thing might be said about the yew Rondel, which appears both too large and over-indebted to the example of Hidcote.

Of course, in the presence of all the roses in full bloom, any perceived defects of design seem unimportant. So let us now slowly wander around the Rose Garden, breathing its scents, enjoying its multifarious scenes, discovering its ever-changing vistas.

In each of the beds described here, the roses take centre stage, complemented by a range of perennial plants, bulbs and some annuals, which create contrast in colour and form – but not too much. Hardy geraniums (up to four different varieties in each bed), corncockles, *Valeriana lecoqii*, sweet peas, monardas, eryngiums, hemerocallis, nicotiana, agapanthus and the smaller

penstemons are key players – but it is essential that these plants do not create too much of a ruckus and upstage the roses. In fact, the varieties here are chosen according to one criterion only: how well they work with the roses. The sweet peas, grown on hazel teepees, are particularly good for this, while their scent is indispensable. Salvias can be strident companions for roses and must be carefully handled; fewer are used today than formerly. Alliums are similarly rationed, as they can overwhelm a garden if unchecked. Familiar plants are grown cheek by jowl with relative rarities; nothing is given the status of 'specimen'. There are always one or two species in there chosen just to keep the wild feeling going – plants such as *Cephalaria gigantea*, *Ammi majus*, *Lunaria* (honesty) and, of course, the foxgloves. In the anthology they edited, entitled *Another World Than This* (1945), Vita and Harold quote Chaucer's *Troilus and Criseyde*, which captures some of the intention.

> *...as ful ofte*
> *Next the foule netle, rough and thikke,*
> *The rose waxeth swote [sweet] and smothe and softe.*

Tall verbascums and eremurus were favoured in Vita's time, and grown against the dark yew Rondel, though today the role of stately foils to the amiable chaos of the roses is largely played by foxgloves (varieties chosen for their muted tones) and a smattering of delphiniums, which Vita loved but tended to reserve for other parts of the garden. Always with tall plants at Sissinghurst, there is the residual memory of the tower which stands at the centre of everything. Clematis is grown on supports to help frame the roses and continue the 'floraison', as Vita called it, after peonies, lupins and other high-summer flowers have faded (a 'dodge' Vita recommended in a BBC talk in the early 1930s). Earlier in the season, the iris collection takes the spotlight. Irises are one of the unsung highlights of Sissinghurst; Vita used to visit the

ABOVE TOP: Penstemon digitalis 'Husker Red' (front), joined by the grey-green foliage of corncockle behind and lit up with Rosa 'Vanity' beyond, with R. 'Tour de Malakoff' (left) and 'Blanche Moreau' (right). ABOVE: The Lutyens bench in front of the Powys Wall, festooned with Clematis 'Perle d'Azur'.

artist and iris breeder Cedric Morris at his art-school home at Benton End in Suffolk, though she would not stay in his house for reasons of hygiene.

Vita was always interested in ground covers, and several are deployed here, some of them interesting in their own right – such as *Waldsteinia ternata* (barren strawberry) and *Phyla nodiflora* – though ordinary epimediums are now the staple, growing alongside old-fashioned primulas and violets. Pinks and pansies play less of a role today than they did in Vita's time, when she declared that she used 'as many pansies as I can get'. These flowers might conceivably look a little strange to modern gardening eyes, but there is perhaps a case for their rehabilitation for historical reasons. Of the old English pinks, Vita delighted in *Dianthus* 'Mrs Sinkins' and also the rarer 'Miss Sinkins'. She mentioned pansies, too, in an article in *Harper's Bazaar* in 1938 in which she paid lavish tribute to William Robinson, the garden stylist to whom she perhaps owed most:

> The real originality of Mr Robinson's methods lay in his choice of what to grow and how to grow it. In his own square beds, for instance, where he grew mostly roses, he also grew clematis, whose purple clusters rose above low shrubs of silvery grey, and he smothered the ground with pansies and low rock-plants.

Late in the season, the asters come out, just to keep some colour interest alive as the roses fade away. There are, incidentally, virtually no ornamental grasses here, or anywhere at Sissinghurst. This is really a garden for late spring and high summer – there is no getting away from it. As Vita commented: 'Plant lavishly and with

LEFT: Grey-green Artemisia ludoviciana *and veronica grow by the path, with roses beyond, including the soft pink 'Felicia' and, against the Powys Wall in the background, 'Purple East'. The bell-flowered* Clematis × diversifolia *is growing on a support (back left).*

concentration on the given moment, and never mind if you get blanks when the moment has passed.'

As for the roses themselves, Vita preferred varieties with simple, strong characteristics that create an impression of authenticity and antiquity. The colour palette was and is based on rich burgundies, magentas, pinks and creams, with a handful of yellow flowers as a counterpoint. Where used, paler yellows are generally favoured – *Rosa* 'Danaë', for example – while round and about there are a few other choice yellows, such as *Hemerocallis* 'Whichford' and 'Corky', and little *Potentilla recta* var. *sulphurea*. During Troy Scott Smith's tenure as head gardener (2013–19) the number of roses in the Rose Garden almost doubled (indeed, many more roses were planted across the entire garden). One effect of this policy is that there are not as many larger shrubs in the Rose Garden as previously – fewer ceanothus and hydrangeas now – but many more perennials squeezed in among the roses. The result is a better balance overall.

Lower plants are encouraged to grow through and around the fragrant, waving antennae of the rose stems, which have to be carefully pruned back now that the garden has so many visitors, and so many pairs of eyes to poke. Vita, of course, hardly pruned at all (except for certain sorts, such as *Rosa gallica* 'Versicolor'). The concept of barely contained chaos was an article of horticultural faith to her until the very last. Her final article on gardening, written for the *Sunday Telegraph* in December 1961, was entitled 'My Roses Thrive on a Touch of Neglect'. Even today the Rose Garden's shrubby effusions explode in front of you at close range, like fragrant floral bombs, a kaleidoscope of rich purple and pink petals, tinged gold and green like the damask for which some of them are named.

In the centre of the garden there are six beds to the west of the Rondel, in the upper rose garden, and four beds to the east, in the lower section. In practice, the adjacent beds meld, with subtle repetitions of species. The plants are not organised in drifts or large clumps but in the cottagey style that Vita championed. The effect is not quite of 'embroidery', which some English gardeners have aimed for, but more of a randomised collage effect. (Any hint of professional organisation will lead to the tone being compromised – which is the single biggest challenge for today's gardeners, who are all, of course, professionals.) The intention is that we should bathe in the garden's luxuriant serendipity – a unifying tone of barely controlled, rampant yet beautiful growth. Neither are they pictorial borders to be viewed down their length, in the classical Arts and Crafts, Jekyllian manner; the garden is more of an immersive experience.

The first bed you encounter (Bed 1 on the plan), immediately to the right on entering from the Top Courtyard, has at its centre four plants of the rich red moss rose 'Célina', surrounded by the graceful pink gallica 'Duchesse d'Angoulême' (first bred in 1821); the magenta gallica 'Tuscany Superb' (raised by nurseryman Thomas Rivers in 1837), whose ancient parent 'Tuscany' Vita said was 'more like the heraldic Tudor rose than any other'; 'Vanity', a deep pink Pemberton hybrid musk rose (bred by the Reverend Pemberton in Essex in the early 20th century); fragrant, pure white 'Blanche Moreau'; and the almost single 'Alain Blanchard', which goes from red to purple. These are only about half the roses in this one bed alone – Sissinghurst's is probably the most important collection of old roses in existence, made all the more irresistible by the romantic story attached to the garden. Many have been chosen as much for their foliage and hips as for their flowers. *Rosa* 'Duplex' (Wolley-Dod's rose), for example, is valued most here for its smoky greyish leaves, a fine foil for flower colour in the pink range.

Bubbling around the roses in this bed are tall plants with a slightly wild aspect – foxgloves and *Delphinium staphisagria*, as well as *Lilium regale*. At a certain point in the 1930s both Harold and Vita fell in love with lilies; one of their big spends early on, in 1934, was on six hundred *L. regale* bulbs. Their taste in plants was usually in alignment, despite Harold's occasional grumblings about Vita's penchant for flowers that are 'brown and difficult to grow'. (On one occasion in 1948 they both visited the same flower show on the same day but did not see each other; they wrote to each other afterwards with exactly the same plant recommendations.)

Bed 1 is filled up with massed plantings of several penstemons: 'Andenken an Friedrich Hahn', with delicate, purple-pink trumpets but not too showy, and white-flowered (despite its name) *Penstemon digitalis* 'Husker Red', with green-purple foliage. Lower down there are hardy geraniums, including *Geranium* x *johnsonii* 'Johnson's Blue', along with some old-fashioned, vivid purple *Heliotropium arborescens* 'Princess Marina', and curiosities such as the little purple-flowered *Tradescantia bracteata*. Also used for ground cover is yellow-flowered *Waldsteinia ternata*, planted beneath the plump box hedges that line the beds. On the theme of box, it has been left to grow rather fatter and shaggier than before, just to emphasise the informal feel of the space. Mauves and purple are the chief colour tones used for the plants beneath and around the roses, though other hues do play their role. Vita was at pains to point out that most of the 'purple' roses in the garden are 'more of a slaty-lilac, like a Parma violet or the breast of a wood-pigeon'. Earlier on, at iris time, 'Blue Boy' (a variety Vita was growing in 1948) and 'Braithwaite' can be found here.

To the left of the path into the Rose Garden from the Top Courtyard is Bed 3, which contains some truly classic old roses: the delicate pink and deliciously scented cabbage rose 'Fantin-Latour', which was rediscovered by one of Vita's rose confederates in the 1940s; crimson-striped 'Variegata di Bologna', bred in Italy in 1909; climbing 'Zéphirine Drouhin' (Vita: 'flowers incessantly but whose strong cherry colour is perhaps a little difficult to place near other things'); the almost purple gallica 'Duc de Guiche', bred in France in 1810 and named in honour of a royalist aristocrat; the rich dark red moss rose 'Nuits de Young' (1845), which was named after Edward Young's cult 18th-century poem *Night Thoughts*; and 'Madame Knorr', a Portland rose with lilac-pink flowers. The rich red flowers of 'William Shakespeare' transform into noteworthy hips. Formerly the alliums (such as *Allium cernuum* and *A. hollandicum*, seen here) played a bigger role in early summer, but a wider range of perennial plants is now used, such as *Penstemon venustus*, the campanula-like *Adenophora potaninii* (ladybells), the spring pea *Lathyrus vernus* 'Alboroseus', characterful geraniums such as *Geranium harveyi*, and also salvias (notably *Salvia* x *sylvestris*) – but not too many.

Peonies were a very 'Vita' plant and are present in the Rose Garden – in this bed there is *Paeonia lactiflora* 'Laura Dessert', with clusters of just-yellow flowers. Muscari and chionodoxa are planted under the peonies to provide early flower colour among its new shoots. Such tonal contrasts as that between 'exotic and expensive' peony and 'cheap and agricultural' cow-parsley types were valued by Vita and are still sought out by the garden team, who are never satisfied with conventional juxtapositions of form and colour, but instead try to keep in mind the essential character of different plants – how their personalities might mingle. For Vita, the idea of using, for example, cardoons or *Melianthus major* as punctuation or architectural plants, was anathema. She preferred more subtle combinations, with plants of different sizes and habits placed together; the common and the rare side by side; the cottagey with the unusual; spire plants with clumpy things; a loose, artless and informal-looking plant found next to something more composed and considered. She would take a sprig of a plant from one part of the garden and place it in another area, as the only way of really seeing whether it worked – a technique the Sissinghurst gardeners still use.

More glamour is provided by the alluring *Lilium* 'Sweet Surrender' with creamy white, almost yellow

ABOVE: The white-flowered Penstemon digitalis *'Husker Red' – rather less demonstrative than other varieties – is among the choice perennials selected to complement the roses.*

petals. Bronze fennel (*Foeniculum vulgare* 'Smoky') produces soft supporting textures, set off by the silver-grey foliage of *Artemisia ludoviciana*. Japanese anemones fill in any gaps in high and late summer, when the soft pink, daisy-flowered *Chrysanthemum* 'Clara Curtis' performs almost like an aster. The anemone is favoured because it never looks as if it is trying too hard, seemingly filling space up naturally. Later in the season, second sowings of annuals and plants such as *Ammi majus*, knautia, sweet rocket (*Hesperis matronalis*) and honesty help to bulk up the late summer scene. The practice with the honesty is for the gardeners to remove by hand the papery coverings to reveal the inner luminous white discs of its flat seed pods, so they sing out in the gloom. It is this attention to detail which raises up the garden. The irises here include the melancholically elegant *Iris ensata* 'Rose Queen', which could have been made for Vita, and the bearded cultivars 'Peggy Chambers' and 'Shannopin' (this last a Harold choice, with striking purple and yellow colouration).

Moving east, the bed next to the Rondel (Bed 5) is larger, with its own collection of venerable shrub roses: the stunning soft pink old rose 'Königin von Dänemark' (raised in Britain in 1826), with fine fragrance; the massive pink, fruitily scented blooms of 'La Ville de Bruxelles' (1836), a damask with handsome leaves; purple-red 'Madame Isaac Péreire' (1881) – which Vita extolled for its early-autumn blooms; 'Japonica', with vivid magenta-pink flowers; and the profuse, sweet pink rambler 'Debutante' (1902). In 2018 three plants each were added of the rugosa roses 'Sarah van Fleet' (1926) – neatly cupped pink flowers with rich yellow stamens; the strongly scented magenta 'Roseraie de l'Hay' (1901); and the pure white 'Blanche Double de Coubert' (1892). It constitutes a rose display of considerable historic interest, but if it is a museum cabinet, it is one of the

LEFT: The Rose Garden in spring, with alliums, valerian and the clear blue Iris 'Placid Waters' (bottom left).

most glorious imaginable. Across these beds trios of *Rosa gallica* 'Versicolor' (rosa mundi) augment the sense of the 'wild' (Vita loved all the variation in the stripy flowers), as well as the moss rose, *Rosa* × *centifolia* 'Muscosa'.

The very 'oldness' of these shrub roses was an attraction in itself, because people of Vita's sensibility will always prize the antique above the new. The paradox is that despite their varietal antiquity (sometimes more apparent than actual), the pleasure of these roses is bound up with their youthfulness, in that each cluster of petals is but a momentary flash of life, shining all too briefly like a glittering dragonfly passing across a sunlit lawn. As the light fades on an early June afternoon, the rich pink blooms seem suffused with honeyed yellows, while the deep red or purple petals harbour unlikely blues and greens amid their thick folds. The whites, yellows and apricots can seem starry and almost fluorescent, or creamily rich, depending on the light and the moment.

Vita recruited white flowers to dramatise the scene, and at least one hundred plants of slender white *Verbascum chaixii* 'Album' can be found in Bed 3. In Vita's time the Rose Garden was celebrated for the way she daringly (for the period) mingled clematis and tall plants, such as verbascums and eremurus, with roses. Jostling with them now are *Agapanthus* 'Kingston Blue', the bridal white *Phlox paniculata* 'Mount Fuji', pink bottlebrushes of *Sanguisorba obtusa* and the elegant, smokily blue-purple-flowered *Campanula* 'Burghaltii'. Vita always enjoyed the sensation of viewing plants at eye level, and alongside the roses are *Clematis* 'Jackmanii' and 'Ville de Lyon' climbing over a tripod frame with spindly *Cephalaria gigantea*, which is less of a horticultural cliché than the over-used *Verbena bonariensis*. At a lower level, there are hostas and the purple mounds of *Strobilanthes attenuata*. Among the irises are 'Amethyst Flame', 'Rosy Veil', golden 'Sahara' and straightforwardly mid-blue 'Tycoon'.

The garden and its central Rondel are bisected by an east-west path that should really be considered more of

a vista than a thoroughfare. In 1972 a decision was made by the National Trust to replace the old mown paths with brick and flagstones; this decisively changed the atmosphere of the Rose Garden, though it was probably unavoidable as Sissinghurst attracted ever more visitors (or pilgrims), and wheelchair access came to be required. But there is perhaps a case for turning the central path back to grass and closing it to visitors. The Rose Garden deserves its green heart, and an inaccessible green path could also intensify the sense of mystery about this place. The box parterre in the White Garden has recently been closed off to visitors and now plays this role – so why not here, too? The flagged paths, meanwhile, provide a fine tonal contrast to foliage, especially that of irises, as Vita opined: 'Stately in their bearing, the irises look their best on either side of a flagged path. The grey of the flat stone sets off both their colour and their contrasting height.' This is nowhere better expressed than in the paths which leave the Rose Garden on its north side.

Moving down into the southern part of the upper rose garden, across this central brick path, Bed 2 in the south-west corner gives us the exuberant pink double rose 'Lavender Lassie'; the demure, blush pink, strongly scented 'Duchesse de Montebello' (1829); and more 'Tuscany Superb'. The wild tone is maintained by means of *Althaea cannabina* (here only; hollyhocks are otherwise omitted at Sissinghurst), astilbes, *Cephalaria alpina* and the remnants of the aquilegia collection. *Monarda* 'Vintage Wine' is used for bulk, and there are daylilies, including *Hemerocallis lilioasphodelus*, 'Night Hawk' and 'Stafford' – though currently the jury is out as to whether they quite fit with the roses. Spring plants include the very old-fashioned *Primula* 'Guinevere', with bronze-green leaves and modest pink flowers, and equally

LEFT: *The north-east corner of the garden, with foaming noisette climbing rose 'Claire Jacquier' on the wall, with the roses 'Madame Lauriol de Barny', 'Kordes' Magenta' and 'Honorine de Brabant' behind* Lupinus 'Jupiter'.

antique, deep purple *Viola* 'Inverurie Beauty'. The tulips throughout this garden have gentle tones, and here we have more modest varieties, such as yellow *Tulipa* 'Cream Perfection' and lily-flowered 'Maytime'. Irises include 'Dorothy' and the haughty little Siberian iris 'Kemugami'.

Bed 4, next door, boasts a deeply scented connoisseur's rose, the old hybrid perpetual 'Baron Girod de l'Ain' (1897): deep red petals fringed with a thin line of white. Chestnut posts have been introduced into the beds to create height, and here *Rosa* 'Debutante' is allowed to perform. Elsewhere the pink ramblers 'Princesse Marie', 'Ethel' and 'Thelma' also clamber around at eye level. On the topic of height, Vita knew and admired the work of Norah Lindsay (whose planting style is maintained by the Trust at Blickling Hall in Norfolk), but her own preference was for more of a profuse, unstructured jumble, as opposed to Lindsay's bubbling continuum punctuated by dramatic evergreen minarets. Vita used height not for architectural effect, but to enhance the feeling of being enveloped in flower and scent. Originally she had crab apples (*Malus* x *purpurea* 'Eleyi') running down the centre of the Rose Garden, but these have been replaced by another Vita favourite, *Prunus* x *subhirtella*, the winter-flowering cherry. In fact, the Rose Garden in Vita's time had a number of other trees, including a paulownia and a pair each of poplars, prunus and cypress; the garden functions more effectively now, with fewer trees.

Other roses in Bed 4 include the ancient red gallica 'Conditorum', which is sometimes known as the Hungarian rose; disarmingly simple *Rosa* 'Lilac Charm', with rich golden stamens; and classic, vigorous 'Cécile Brünner' (1881), 'the sweetheart rose', sporting clusters of delicate blooms where the petals always look as if they are on the point of falling off. The spires of gently violet-blue-flowered *Salvia pratensis* Haematodes Group — less demonstrative than others of this genus — mingle with the rose stems, foliage and blooms. *Anthericum ramosum*, with white star flowers, has the air of a wild flower, jangling with the spiky thistles of *Eryngium variifolium*. Others in the supporting cast include catmint, delicate *Phlox stolonifera* 'Mary Belle Frey', *Gazania* 'Cream Beauty' and the decadently pink *Anemone hupehensis* var. *japonica* 'Prinz Heinrich'. On the theme of decadence, there are more peonies here, notably rich red *Paeonia lactiflora* 'Karl Rosenfield'. Lower down is *Primula* 'Guinevere', again, in addition to a collection of violas, including *Viola* 'Ivory White', and ground-covering *Phyla nodiflora*, which goes by the delightful name of frogfruit. Late spring offers the superior *Iris* 'Broadleigh Rose' and *I.* 'Pink Clover', with luscious orange-pink petals.

Bed 6, by the Rondel on the south side, includes a rose that was particularly special to Vita, as she felt — with some justification — that she had personally rehabilitated it. She described how she had spotted the rich maroon flowers of 'Souvenir du Docteur Jamain' 'growing against the office-wall in a somewhat derelict nursery. They had no stock, and had no interest, and said I could have the plant if I liked to take the risk of moving it. I took the risk; it succeeded; and I have had the pleasure of restoring it (as I believe) to circulation.' This hybrid perpetual was the creation, in 1865, of the Lyonnais breeder François Lacharme. It is the most richly coloured rose in the bed; the others are lighter in tone and include classic 'Félicité Parmentier' (1834), with the freshest and brightest pink flowers imaginable; 'Buff Beauty', with distinctive apricot blooms; and the stately Pemberton rose 'Penelope' — simple white flowers lifted by prominent yellow stamens, with a scent Vita valued as much as any other. In addition, at least ten *Rosa gallica* var. *officinalis* intensify that artfully overgrown feeling. There

RIGHT: Stars of the Rose Garden: 'Penelope' (top left); 'Président de Sèze' (top right); 'Souvenir du Docteur Jamain' (middle left); 'Ethel' (bottom left); and 'Guirlande d'Amour' in the evening light (bottom right).

are also a few surprises, such as fiery orange *Hemerocallis fulva* 'Green Kwanso' and *Mahonia nervosa*. Here are more peonies, plus the sweet little *Polemonium carneum* 'Apricot Delight'. A group of *Iris* Californian hybrids, the gift of Sarah Raven, is planted beneath an osmanthus.

On the other (east) side of the yew Rondel, in the lower rose garden, are four beds, slightly less rambunctious than those already described. To the north, next to the Rondel, is Bed 7, with another specimen of the pink rambler rose 'Thelma' on a post and *Clematis* 'Prince Charles' on a frame, surrounded by white, repeat-flowering *Rosa* 'Blush Noisette' (or 'Noisette Carnée', 1817); 'Mrs Oakley Fisher' – single yolk-yellow flowers (a typically challenging Vita choice); the bright pink moss rose 'Salet' (1854); and the wild, luxuriantly spreading 'Dunwich Rose', apparently rediscovered in 1950 growing on sand dunes in Suffolk, hence its name. There is an underplanting of variegated *Brunnera macrophylla* 'Dawson's White', and the wildflower-like *Eurybia divaricata* helps maintain the tone, while one notably bohemian iris here is 'Benton Nigel', with big floppy petals (it was 'one of Cedric's', of course).

Bed 9, next door on the north side, features *Rosa* 'Président de Sèze' (1836), of which a specialist nursery once noted: 'variously described as cerise, violet and silvery grey, the overall effect being of lilac-pink', together with *Agapanthus* 'Loch Hope', *Geranium clarkei* 'Kashmir White' and *Platycodon grandiflorus*, with blue star-flowers. Sweet peas are a near-constant presence among the roses, and here we have the shamelessly tutti-frutti *Lathyrus odoratus* 'Heirloom Bicolour Mixed'.

Immediately to the south-east of the Rondel, Bed 8 features another *Rosa* 'Thelma' on a post, along with the creamily pink moss rose 'Alfred de Dalmas' (1855),

LEFT: Iris 'Melchior' (above) and 'Shannopin' (below) are both varieties favoured by Vita and Harold and can be seen in the Rose Garden today.

deep purple 'Cardinal de Richelieu' (1845) and more 'Président de Sèze'. Alongside traditional cottage plants, such as *Campanula lactiflora* 'Loddon Anna' and *Geranium* 'Spinners', we find the intriguing *Paris polyphylla*, with its splayed leaves, and the equally complex *Tricyrtis* 'Adbane'.

Bed 10, in the south-east corner of the Rose Garden, is dominated by *Rosa* 'Ulrich Brünner Fils' (1881), one of the hybrid perpetuals Vita favoured, with shapely crimson blooms, supported by groups of the pink-striped 'Ferdinand Pichard' (1921) and 'Souvenir du Docteur Jamain'. Amid the Japanese anemones (*Anemone* x *hybrida* 'Honorine Jobert') and fragile-looking *Penstemon* 'Alice Hindley', *Fuchsia* 'Sealand Prince' comes as a pleasant surprise. It is one of the eccentricities of the Rose Garden, perhaps, but Vita liked and recommended certain fuchsias for the 'ecclesiastical' appeal of their flowers. This variety is a full-on fuchsia, not a polite one of the sort chosen by people who fear they may be thought vulgar. Vita disdained that attitude more, even, than perceived vulgarity itself. In fact, such floral shocks were always viewed as a necessity (an attitude energetically pursued, later, by 'Christo' Lloyd at Great Dixter). Vita had a penchant, for example, for striped and brightly coloured zinnias. (They were tried again in the Moat Walk in 2016 but fell prey to snails emerging from the walls.)

The beds around the Rondel may be the heart of the Rose Garden, but there is more to come from the wide border against the garden's north wall – the closest Sissinghurst comes to a traditional long border. More shrubs are here, with ceanothus and a fig playing a key role in the north-western corner, and abelia, kolkwitzia (a shrub Vita eulogised over) and clerodendrum deployed elsewhere. The roses are also slightly shrubbier and wilder-looking, overall, with striped rosa mundi and the classic mid-pink *Rosa* 'Kew Rambler'. Perennial effects in this far corner (Bed 11) come from *Centaurea dealbata* 'Steenbergii', the soft purple *Trachelium caeruleum* and the wildflower-like *Morina longifolia*. Among the irises are (west to east) 'Melchior' (a variety Vita was growing here in 1948), 'Jane Phillips', 'Cleo', 'London Pride', 'Blue Rhythm', 'Deputé Nomblot' and 'Green Ice'.

Bed 12, the central section, has the wild roses *Rosa glauca* and *R. nutkana* 'Plena' (an original Vita planting), 'Königin von Dänemark', and 'Paul's Lemon Pillar' (1915), with a strong, sweet fragrance. This last was a favourite of Vita's, who extolled not just its scent and flower – 'so subtle a colour that one does not know whether to call it ivory or sulphur or iceberg green' – but also its buds, which are possessed of 'a sculptural quality which suggests curled shavings of marble, if one may imagine marble made of the softest ivory suede'. The roses are bolstered by acanthus, crinum lilies, foxgloves, *Eucomis pallidiflora*, orange *Sphaeralcea munroana*, and the fluffy white flowers of *Anaphalis margaritacea* var. *yedoensis*. The fancy mint *Lepechinia floribunda* adds further intrigue, with *Nerine bowdenii* following on in autumn. More *Iris* 'Cleo' grows here, a variety Vita was cultivating in 1948.

There are a few roses with choice characteristics in Beds 13 and 14, at the eastern end of the big, south-facing border: the highly scented flowers of 'Belle de Crécy' (1829), a rich cherry pink that fades to soft violet; the silvery pink flowers of 'Madame Lauriol de Barny' (1868), which are held in an elegant quatrefoil pattern; the green rose, *R.* x *odorata* 'Viridiflora' (1845), a sport of the classic china rose 'Pallida' ('Old Blush'); and 'Reine des Violettes' (1860) with, as the name suggests, flowers in a range of soft purple hues, shading to magenta. Then there is the simple white *Rosa* 'White Wings', with rich red centres; golden *R.* x *harisonii* 'Williams' Double Yellow' (old yellow Scotch rose); and the fresh violet-pink moss rose 'Général Kléber' (named after one of Napoleon's generals). Pemberton rose 'Danaë' has flouncy yellow flowers fading to cream.

These plants are complemented by crinum lilies, *Nicotiana langsdorffii*, *Crambe cordifolia*, *Kniphofia* 'Lemon

Ice' and the filigree-petalled *Catananche caerulea*, with *Salvia uliginosa*, *Betonica macrantha* and *Geranium renardii* 'Whiteknights' also performing their duty. White *Dicentra formosa* f. *alba* runs through, adding that naturalistic feel which is such an important tonal element at Sissinghurst.

All of Sissinghurst's roses are pruned quite hard, and the garden team reckon on at least two thousand hours to get the job done. Massive bender structures made of hazel are used in the eastern beds, a system whose genesis Vita accredited to her long-serving head gardener, Jack Vass (who had brought the technique with him from Cliveden). In the Rose Garden as elsewhere the matter of pruning is prioritised as a key horticultural skill. The job begins on 15 October, starting with the ramblers and climbers around South Cottage. Then all the other roses in the garden are tackled – which includes retraining them against the walls. It is only after Christmas that the gardeners finally attack (in the nicest possible way) the Rose Garden itself. The wall roses are done first, simply because it is safer to use ladders while it is not as cold and windy. Sissinghurst's heavy clay soil means that the garden is often waterlogged in winter, so wooden boards are used to cross areas of earth in the beds. Aesthetically, it is interesting how the protective cloak of mainly oak trees which envelops the garden (and makes it feel old) plays a more pronounced role in the winter months. The two avenues of poplars – one at the entrance and the other leading to the Lake – are also much more prominent at this time.

The border on the south side of the Rose Garden is somewhat curtailed due to the unorthodox shape of the space, where it meets the edge of the Lime Walk. A very old rose can be found at the far western end, by the Powys Wall (Bed 20): *Rosa* 'Celsiana', dating back to the 18th century or earlier, with clusters of pale pink flowers offset by golden stamens (it is also a long-flowerer). Near to it is the gallica 'Nestor' (1834), which boasts dignified, tightly petalled, lilac-pink flowers that turn almost grey

at the outer edges. In the shadier eastern section we find hellebores, together with masses of *Pulmonaria saccharata* 'Frühlingshimmel' and *Saxifraga* 'Miss Chambers'. *Lilium* 'Attila' sings out among *Eryngium bourgatii* and *Incarvillea delavayi*, while *Fuchsia* 'Chillerton Beauty' and *Hemerocallis* 'Whichford' also have their moments.

The central section (Bed 17) of the south border is dominated by seven 'Sissinghurst Castle' roses, alongside *Rosa* 'Madame Hardy' (1832) – strong white blooms with small green centres; *R. x centifolia* 'Shailer's White Moss' (1784); the Pemberton musk rose 'Nur Mahal' (1923), with bright purple-crimson flowers and golden stamens; and the wild rose 'Mary, Queen of Scots', featuring small, double flowers of purple and lilac-grey, paler on the outside. There are more hellebores and pulmonarias, as well as the lilac *Syringa × prestoniae* 'Elinor'.

Bed 16, just south-east of the Rondel, is crammed with roses, including more 'Madame Hardy'; 'Belle de Crécy'; and the graceful species rose *Rosa willmottiae*, underplanted with *Dryopteris* ferns and hellebores. White foxgloves contrast dynamically with the dark foliage of *Sambucus nigra*. Here, too, is the Scotch briar rose 'Stanwell Perpetual' (1838), which Vita valued for its 'sweet-scented, double flowers of the palest shell-pink used for picking bowls you can plunge your nose into…it is truly perpetual, non-stop; I have picked stray blooms right up to the first frosts.' On the topic of scent, Vita observed that modern roses 'may smell rich and sweet at close quarters, but few of them spread their fragrance on the air', whereas the old roses she preferred are 'those that catch you as you walk past'.

The Rose Garden is the most intense, romantic and frankly hedonistic of Sissinghurst's spaces. Vita claimed she was 'drunk on roses' – and here, we can be, too. 🐝

RIGHT: The low-growing Rosa spinosissima *'William III' with the 'Shannopin' iris beyond, by the path to the Top Courtyard.*

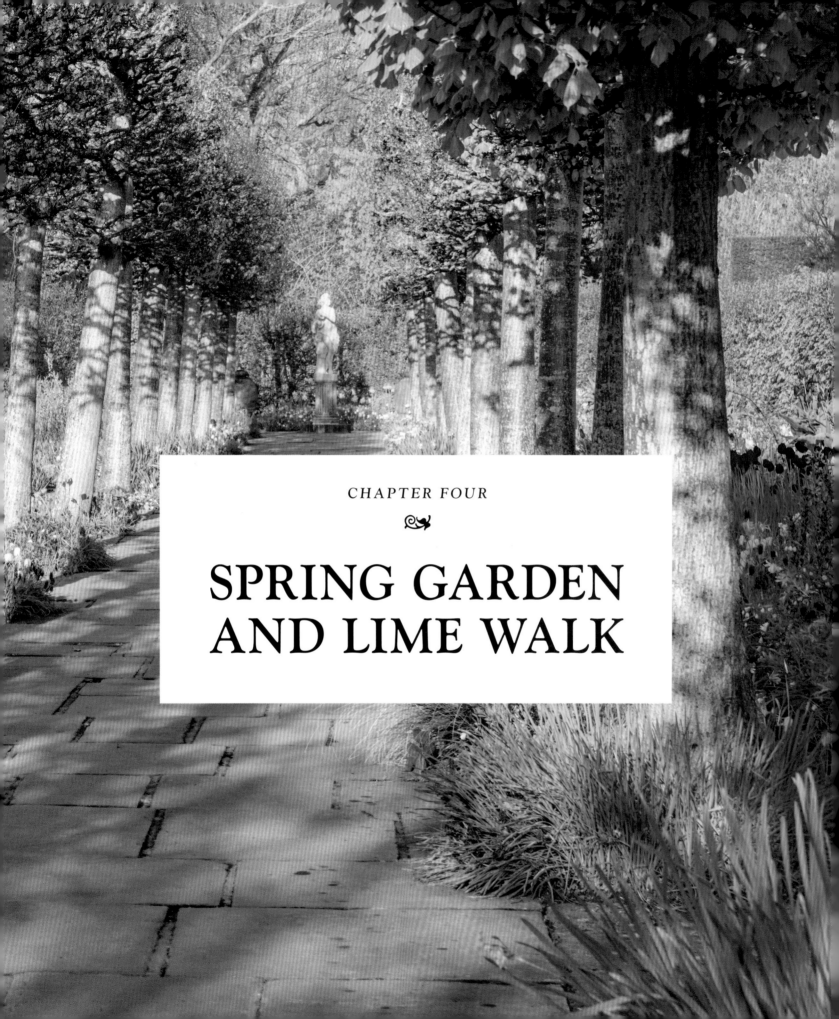

CHAPTER FOUR

SPRING GARDEN AND LIME WALK

'I believe that before we die we shall make
Sissinghust the loveliest garden in Kent.
And we can only do this by getting better
and better varieties of things we like. . .
there are certain things which are adapted
to Sissingbags and those things should be
improved and improved and improved until
they reach the perfect standard.'

🌹 Letter from Harold Nicolson to
Vita Sackville-West, 15 May 1946

THIS WAS HAROLD'S own place. A long bower bathed in the fresh green of the pleached lime trees which flank the pathway, doubly hemmed by clipped hornbeam hedges. This sweetly meditative tunnel is, of course, designed to be at its best in the springtime, with bright plantings of tulips, narcissi, scillas and primulas lining the path, and views down and into the mysterious, ferny Nuttery at the far east end.

The Spring Garden, with its central Lime Walk, was the one part of the garden where Harold designed not only the structure but also the planting. He even employed his own personal gardener to work here. As a result it has a slightly different feel to the rest of Sissinghurst. But it plays its role at the edge of things, this intriguing road to nowhere.

It was in November 1932 that Harold and Vita laid out the lines of the Lime Walk and planted the hornbeam hedges behind. The thirty lime trees were planted in 1936, when the walk was also paved. The western end is focused on a statue of a cymbal-playing Bacchante,

PREVIOUS PAGE: The Spring Garden in its April pomp, looking west towards the twirling Bacchante statue. LEFT: The view east towards the Nuttery, through the fresh green of the pleached lime leaves.

an ecstatic female follower of Bacchus or Dionysus – whom we shall meet at the other end of the garden, by the Moat. Harold organised it so that there is a north-south vista all the way from the middle of the White Garden (the original rose garden), right across Tower Lawn, through the doorway into the Rose Garden (the vegetable garden as was), down the centre of the yew Rondel, and thence into the Spring Garden and Lime Walk with its twirling Bacchante, set on the base of a column. It is one of three or four principal vistas which untidily parcel up the garden.

The trees were replaced in 1977, with *Tilia platyphyllos* 'Rubra' instead of Harold's suckering common limes. (A slight change in the position of the limes means that Harold's original dimensions have also been altered.) Vita decried Harold's habit of pruning the limes himself while precariously perched on a ladder, suggesting that he was a 'physical imbecile', as Harold jokily relayed in a letter to his sons. (He fell off the ladder several times.) Today, the pleaching is done more safely and is harder on the inner side, for a crisp effect.

Harold's ambition here was for a colourful promenade of alpine and other spring flowers, which he named Unter den Linden in honour of Berlin's most

rejuvenated once the paint had been washed off the slabs by rain. Sometimes people are surprised that so much concrete was used in the garden. This was purely for economic reasons. Vita and Harold were never rich (though they had their moments with book advances and also inherited a considerable sum from Vita's mother, Lady Sackville) and Harold's diaries and letters are peppered with references to unpaid bills and income tax demands. He tended to take these seriously, while Vita, of course, never did. They did have to economise in some ways: they bought most of their statuary and architectural fragments from cheap antique stalls and used the concrete (or, more usually, a mix of concrete and stone) for some paths when York stone would have been preferred. But the reality was that financial problems were for them an irritation rather than a potentially life-changing dilemma.

Vita avoided mentioning Harold's German inspiration in her 1953 article about the garden in the RHS *Journal*, instead conjuring the image of 'a spring garden suggesting the foreground of Botticelli's *Primavera*', with anemones, muscari, *Omphalodes luciliae*, chionodoxas, *Iris pumila*, *Tulipa dasystemon* and erythroniums. The bulbs tend to struggle in the heavy clay soil, but Harold persevered over many years. The ingredients of the Spring Garden became an abiding interest for him, as evinced by a series of planning notebooks he kept from 1946 until the late 1950s. His particular favourites were spring flowers of simpler character, such as the jonquils, primroses, violets, scillas and small tulips like 'Clara Butt'. Within that range he pursued scores of varieties, making the planting different every year. A series of large Tuscan terracotta jars was later interspersed under

fashionable avenue. (It had also been a well-known gay cruising ground since the early 19th century – possibly a private joke by Harold.) He had come to know the city when posted to Germany as a diplomat in the late 1920s, and its destruction during the war was a matter of profound regret to him. After his political career had finally come to an end in 1945, when he lost his parliamentary seat in the election, Harold referred to the Spring Garden and Lime Walk as 'My Life's Work', or 'MLW' for short.

One slightly bizarre detail is that Harold originally installed a painted multicoloured (pink, green, yellow) pathway of concrete slabs running down the middle of the limes; perhaps fortunately, this feature was not

ABOVE: The focal statue is a Bacchante, a pleasure-seeking female follower of Bacchus. RIGHT: The Nuttery end of the Lime Walk, with fragrant Hyacinthus orientalis *'Delft Blue' and* Tulipa sylvestris *behind. The dark purple* Fritillaria persica *towers behind the narcissi.*

the limes down the length of the garden, with a pair flanking the Bacchante statue. *Rosa pimpinellifolia* has been replanted against the hornbeam hedge to provide structure, as it was in Harold's time, alongside forsythia, brooms and *Rosa rugosa*.

The Spring Garden's tapestry is still characterised by a profusion of scillas, fritillaries, bluebells and primulas, with the addition of numerous narcissi and tulips in succession. Around the Bacchante is a planting of *Alchemilla mollis,* with the likes of *Anemone nemorosa, Fritillaria imperialis* and *Muscari latifolium.* Narcissi here include 'Charity May', 'Tête-à-Tête' and 'Dove Wings', and a cast of tulips: 'Ballerina', 'Generaal de Wet', 'Orange Emperor', 'Bronze Charm'. On the north side of the Lime Walk, at its western end, we have *Crocus tommasinianus* leading in to groups of *Anemone nemorosa* 'Allenii', *Scilla messeniaca* and fritillaries such as *F. persica* 'Adiyaman' and *F. acmopetala.* The backdrop includes *Prunus tenella* 'Fire Hill' and *Euphorbia epithymoides* 'Major'. The middle of this northern side is characterised by masses of *Mertensia virginica* (Virginia bluebells) and other fritillaries, while the tulip mix is augmented by *T. saxatilis* and *T. kolpakowskiana.* The southern side of the Lime Walk reprises the same bulbous themes, with swathes of *Scilla litardierei* and *S. messeniaca,* and narcissi such as 'Actaea' and 'Minnow', backed by fresh green-yellow cushions of *Euphorbia epithymoides.* But it is not a mirror-image effect across the central path; there is constant variation. The terracotta pots, however, are all planted identically with the same ingredients, which might be fritillaries, primulas, phlox and anemones, with the orange-red species tulip *T. orphanidea,* underplanted with *Alchemilla conjuncta* or *Sanicula epipactis.*

RIGHT: The tulip mix in the giant terracotta pots often echoes that of the Top Courtyard, and features here 'Negrita', 'Ronaldo' and 'Havran'.

The Spring Garden and Lime Walk presents a definitive contrast with the Rose Garden, by which most visitors enter. In fact, this straight green corridor, with its intimations of infinity, has a decidedly surreal air – though the surrealism of Sissinghurst, with its long passages and abrupt turns, is of a very English sort, owing more to the jaunty pastoral picaresque of *Alice in Wonderland* than the sinister reversals of René Magritte. Throughout the garden, scale is distorted (in the plantings, as well as in the overall layout) so that the visitor feels pleasantly disorientated for much of the time.

The influence of Hidcote, Lawrence Johnston's garden in Gloucestershire, has already been remarked upon in the context of Sissinghurst. The Rose Garden and its Rondel are, structurally, perhaps the most Hidcotian part of the garden, but the Spring Garden seems similarly indebted. Yet there are salient differences between these two great gardens, which are so often mentioned in the same breath (and it should be an Arts and Crafts triumvirate, with Rodmarton, that true expression of William Morris's ideals, as the third).

Sissinghurst has none of the poise and rhythm of Hidcote, where everything seems felicitously balanced and spaces segue into each other deftly and with panache. Sissinghurst works in quite another way – proceeding in an illogical manner, with several abrupt or uncertain transitions (around the Cottage Garden, for example, where no entrance or exit is clear-cut). Yet that is all part of its charm and character. Sissinghurst is a place of slight misalignments and joyful moments. Like Vita and Harold themselves, it is congenitally skew-whiff. Mr and Mrs Nicolson of Sissinghurst made a garden in which to express themselves, whereas Mr Johnston of Hidcote made a garden in which to hide himself. The garden at Sissinghurst seems to erupt around the visitor like a sparkling conversation, of the kind in which its progenitors excelled, with new ideas tumbling out,

contradictions leading to unexpected avenues and vistas, and sometimes unheralded moments of stasis.

The most useful lesson Harold learned from Ned Lutyens, who went to visit and advise for a day when they were living at Long Barn, was the importance of making garden spaces or 'rooms' that were large enough. (Lutyens visited Sissinghurst only once, in 1936, by which time Harold had laid out the bones of the garden.) Problems of scale typically beset amateur garden designers, and one of Harold's great successes lay in avoiding that trap. He was, after all, a descendant of the celebrated 18th-century architect Robert Adam. Nevertheless, his layout for Sissinghurst is not a masterclass in expert garden design in every respect. A skilled professional like Lutyens, or Harold Peto, or Robert Weir Schultz, would have laid out the garden rationally as a sequence of spaces that flow into one another. There would have been a sense of ascending and descending hierarchy in terms of the sizes and shapes of the garden's spaces, and there would have been a strong emphasis on the interstitial areas, the engineering of the link passages between the episodes. Not so at Sissinghurst. Harold's design is full of sudden expansions and contractions; the scale seems to be all over the place and, when seen on plan, none of the lines and demarcations in the garden makes any sense.

But how well it works on the ground! It is its very eccentricity and spontaneity which sets it apart. Harold's instinctive decision-making has resulted in a garden whose layout seems to mimic the development of human emotions across a single day, as if Virginia Woolf's novel *Mrs Dalloway*, with its stream-of-consciousness narration, had been remade in garden form (see Interlude chapter for an analysis of Sissinghurst's quasi-literary effects).

RIGHT: Spring Garden delights: leucojum (top left); potted narcissi – the tallest one is 'Martinette' – with pink chaenomeles in the urn behind (top right); Scilla messeniaca *(middle left);* Fritillaria imperialis *(bottom left); and the woodlander* Fothergilla major *(bottom right).*

ABOVE: Tulips, including 'Gavota' (maroon and yellow) and 'Shirley' (at the back, white edged with purple) are backed by the elegant Fritillaria persica.

The alpine-tapestry planting of the Spring Garden and Lime Walk has something of the jauntiness of Harold himself, who was possessed of an irrepressible and armour-plated personality, outwardly at least. Vita recalled her first impressions of her husband-to-be: 'I liked his irrepressible brown curls, his laughing eyes, his charming smile, and his boyishness.' One of Harold's most appealing diary entries, which rather sums up his style and character, was made in the spring of 1932, when he and Vita were gardening like mad at Sissinghurst. 'I cannot get a job and am deeply in debt. I foresee no exit from our financial worries. Yet Vita and I are as happy as larks alone together. It is a spring day. Very odd.'

Harold was educated at public school (Wellington College) and then Balliol College, Oxford, an institution which famously produced 'men of the world', specialising in politicians. Yet reading one of Harold's blockbuster historical works, such as *The Age of Reason* (1960), you realise that he was not possessed of what is known in Oxford as 'a first-class mind'; there are no original or striking insights to be found. His abiding talent was for friendship and clubbability. Harold was able to turn his skills to the public benefit in his role as a diplomat, a profession that fitted him like a glove.

It only started to go wrong for him when he went into politics, which does not tend to reward honesty – and Harold was instinctively honest. He also lacked ruthlessness, while at the same time succumbing to idealism rather too readily – hence his unwise dalliance with Oswald Mosley's New Party in 1931, before it morphed into the British Union of Fascists. (He edited *Action*, the party's weekly house magazine, which is where, incidentally, Vita's very first articles on gardening appeared, including a column on roses in the 29 October issue.) Later, Harold found success as MP for West Leicester from 1935 to 1945, having stood as a member of the small National Labour Party, which was nominally allied with the Conservatives. He redeemed his earlier association with Mosley by warning of the dangers of Hitler and standing against the appeasement policy with Churchill. His finest moment came in 1938: a speech in Parliament against Chamberlain's Munich Agreement.

Honesty, idealism, a lack of ruthlessness – these are all defects in a politician. It explains Winston Churchill's relations with him, as relayed in Harold's diary. Churchill regarded Harold warily as a rather mysterious, guileless sort of person who deserved to be admired and pitied in equal measure.

Harold was a social animal who loved London life and his cronies at the Travellers Club, while Vita became increasingly allergic to the metropolis. That is one of the reasons why Sissinghurst is considered to be more Vita's creation than Harold's. She occupied the place so intensely that it seemed indivisible from her being, whereas Harold viewed his country house more in the classical tradition of 'rural retreat', so redolent of the 18th century – a place for relaxation away from the busyness of city life and court, where one's physical and moral batteries could be recharged. Indeed, at Harold's memorial service in 1968, John Sparrow, warden of All Souls College, Oxford, speculated that he was 'a 19th-century character living an 18th-century life in the middle of the 20th century'.

The son of a diplomat, Harold was born in Tehran and may have felt somewhat rootless all his life. In *The Desire to Please* (1943), a biography of his great-great-grandfather, he remarked: 'The Nicolsons have for many generations been a landless tribe.' Perhaps this is why Sissinghurst meant so much to him. Yet even at Sissinghurst he felt a little extraneous at times, lamenting, 'the bore about it is that I love Viti's taste – and never wish in reality to depart from it. Only I want a room of my own.' This private whinge is also a sly little reference to Virginia Woolf's proto-feminist essay 'A Room of One's Own'. (Ultimately, Harold did manage to build a room for himself; it was tacked on to the South Cottage.)

There may have been a legal and financial aspect to this inequality of sense of ownership: on paper at least, Vita owned Sissinghurst in its entirety.

As for Vita, she loved Harold – or 'Hadji' ('pilgrim') as his father had nicknamed him – for 'his brain and his delicious disposition'. She wrote that she saw him 'far more as a playfellow than in any other light. Our relationship was so fresh, so intellectual, so unphysical, that I never thought of him in that aspect at all.' Perhaps it is in part this atmosphere of 'play', and the somewhat semi-detached nature of Harold and Vita's relationship, which gives the garden its lively and spontaneous feel even today. It came naturally to them both to make an illusory miniature world of high gestures and intimate moments, as a kind of salve against reality. It is this world into which we are poured, as goggle-eyed visitors.

Sissinghurst is extolled as the product of a marriage of equals working in harmony, but this only came about as a result of a strict division of responsibility: Harold worked out the ground plan, and had the Spring Garden and Lime Walk as his own, while Vita did everything else. They chose sculpture and architectural materials together, but when it came to planting, Vita ruled. Harold had his opinions on plants, which he did advance from time to time – but Vita won nearly all those battles. The only horticultural skirmish from which he emerged as victor was with regard to rhododendrons, which were banished from the main garden at his request – though Vita planted plenty down by the Lake.

Predictably, it was not all plain sailing within this *ménage à trois* of wife, husband and garden. This is a type of relationship with which many gardening couples will be familiar, since the garden often functions as the

LEFT: Some thirty different varieties of aster, in a range of mauves and purples, take over the planting of the Lime Walk in late summer.

third element in a marriage. Harold's diary entry for 29 December 1946 reads:

In the afternoon I moon about with Vita trying to convince her that planning is an element in gardening. I want to show her that the top of the moat-walk bank must be planted with forethought and design. She wishes just to jab in the things which she has left over. The tragedy of the romantic temperament is that it dislikes form so much that it ignores the effect of masses. She wants to put in stuff which 'will give a lovely red colour in the autumn'. I wish to put in stuff which will furnish shape to the perspective. In the end we part, not as friends.

The irony is that, although Vita won most of the garden battles, it was her vision (horticultural) that inevitably proved most ephemeral, and which the National Trust now struggles to recreate. Harold's layout (architectural), on the other hand, has endured virtually intact. The garden still oscillates between their influences.

There has also been a tendency to couch the division of labour at Sissinghurst in terms of gender – the sexual stereotyping of Vita doing the 'soft' planting, Harold in charge of the 'hard' structure. Given the sexual orientation and character of those involved, this analysis seems even more fatuous than usual. Gardens allow men and women to transcend their culturally ascribed roles. Sissinghurst stands as an emblem of the blurring of gender distinction, not its tacit reinforcement. Harold and Vita's son Nigel Nicolson noticed 'the interplay of male and female characteristics in each of them', while Vita, comfortable with the notion of fluid sexuality from an early stage of life, would have concurred with these thoughts about Orlando (and, indeed, Woolf may have been quoting directly from her in her novel): 'Different though the sexes are, they intermix. In every human being a vacillation from one sex to the other takes place, and often it is only the clothes that keep the male or female likeness.'

This was something that was played out in the garden – literally played out, for the garden was their plaything, as well as the most intense expression of their artistic lives. It was the physical fruition of the unconventional private reality of their marriage, their children being the fruition of its more conventional, public aspect. (Harold's response, on being asked by a journalist whether he and his wife had ever collaborated on anything, was to observe that they had produced two children.) The painful truth is that in certain important ways, the garden they had made clearly meant more to Harold and Vita than their children did. It was, after all, a more authentic expression of the nature of their partnership. Any realisation of this must have been difficult for Nigel and Ben to assimilate, and perhaps helps explain Nigel's decision to reveal all in print about his parents' marriage after their deaths.

Gardens are as much about the invisible as the visible. What is felt. Those few steps from the Rose Garden into the Spring Garden circumscribe the relationship which gave rise to this extraordinary place. 🦋

RIGHT: Early spring, when the pleached trees create their own architecture and mature clumps of leucojum appear. .

CHAPTER FIVE

THE NUTTERY

'So in this cave of watered green
Cool all thy thoughts by care opprest,
And let the sunlight fall between
The leaves, and dapple on thy breast.'

🌹 Invitation to Cast Out Care by
Vita Sackville-West, 1931

FROM THE RATIONAL certainty of the dead-straight Lime Walk, the visitor enters the mysterious, shadowy realm of the Nuttery. What is most noticeable about the transition is a change in the quality of light, a different tone of green – from the openness and multicoloured floral displays of the Spring Garden, and the lime-light of the pleach, into the deeper green simplicity of the shade cast by the hazel coppice. In spring this is accentuated by the limpid, soft green light seemingly thrown up by the young shuttlecock ferns. Structurally, the Nuttery acts as a kind of buffer zone between more formal episodes – the Spring Garden and the Herb Garden to west and east, with the vibrant azaleas of the Moat Walk lighting up its northern boundary.

The nut trees are a continuation, of sorts, of the lime tree avenue in the Spring Garden and Lime Walk. They are about the same size, but are of quite a different character. Harold thinned them out on arrival so they almost, but not quite, became an avenue (the 'almost' in that sentence being an indication of good design, not bad). Their coppiced stems give them an untidy feel compared with the Gallic propriety of the lime pleach, while at their bases, an erupting woodland understorey of fresh greenery and flowers further blurs any impression of a formal axis. All of this is deliberate, and effective.

The Nuttery, a non-garden set in the midst of many and various little gardens, creates one of the moments of disorientation which are so integral to the Sissinghurst experience. It could almost be labelled a quixotic feature, this shady realm on the sunniest side of the garden, a miniature woodland in which there is nothing to do but get lost.

The Nuttery was what drew Vita and Harold to Sissinghurst in the first place. Or it was the clincher, at least. As Harold wrote in his diary entry after their second visit: 'We then go round the buildings carefully and finally walk round the fields to the brook and round by the wood. We come suddenly upon a nut walk and that settles it.' With the tower looming over them, beckoning to Vita as if from a childhood dream, it was impossible that they would not buy Sissinghurst – though Harold did try, briefly, to be sensible, arguing that it was all too expensive and burdensome.

PREVIOUS PAGE: The most mysterious part of the garden, it was the discovery of the overgrown Nuttery that persuaded Vita and Harold to buy Sissinghurst Castle. OPPOSITE: The hazels are coppiced for decorative reasons today, creating a temple-like setting for the statue of Bacchus. Scilla messeniaca and fritillaries carpet the scene.

Harold, in particular, was delighted to find the hazel coppice, almost covered over by brambles and weeds. Optimistically, he had first described it as a 'nut walk' and later they attempted to rename it the Nut Plat, an old Kentish term which never quite stuck. The idea of a nuttery appealed to them, as an orchard did, because they approved of the notion that a garden could be – ought to be – productive and beautiful at one and the same time. What gardeners of Vita and Harold's background were (and are) most fearful of is accusations of pretension or trying too hard; the Nuttery plays another supporting role in that it feeds into the idea of Sissinghurst as a farm of sorts. That is the feeling that their grandson, Adam Nicolson, has been trying to reintroduce in recent years. Vita cherished anything that typified the Kentish Weald, and a nuttery fitted the mould – the coppice's most important harvest being its rods (strong, slender, pliable branches), as opposed to the nuts.

The rest of Sissinghurst was in many ways quite a difficult and depressing prospect when Vita and Harold arrived – though there was always the tower in the centre as its beating romantic heart, and the charmingly domestic South Cottage as a bonus. The Nuttery was the only part of the garden that seemed to them to have retained some of its own horticultural character and, in truth, it was the only part which then seemed to show any faint twitches of life. It would become the focus of their initial efforts at resuscitation – one of the first things they did in 1930 was to clear it, along with the adjacent Moat Walk.

The unsung and unassuming Nuttery may be described, therefore, as the earliest element of the horticultural extravaganza we enjoy today at Sissinghurst.

For Harold, the orientation of the Nuttery also created a design problem – which he characteristically turned to the garden's advantage. His original idea was for a long vista from the Rose Garden, down through the Nuttery. But the nuts had been planted (probably in around 1900) in rows which were not in alignment with this axis. So he scrapped that idea and linked his new Lime Walk instead with the Nuttery, the vista ending in an uncertain dissolve amid the greenery of the ferns. This is most effective and also forms a satisfying contrast with other Sissinghurst views, most of which end in a small statue or architectural fragment. (Decorative urns were not favoured, probably because of that underlying fear of pretension; they generally look best in larger acreages.) One garden particularly admired by Harold was St Paul's Walden Bury, in Hertfordshire, an 18th-century garden of vistas cut through woodland revealing small peeping ornaments and fragmentary glimpses of architecture. There is something of that flavour at Sissinghurst.

For Harold, then, the Nuttery was a design conundrum. For Vita, its appeal was, of course, more romantic, if not metaphysical. Her novel *Family History* was published in 1932, shortly after they came to Sissinghurst. It includes a vivid portrait of the garden as the setting for an intense love affair between Miles (who is Vita, in actuality) and Evelyn. At one point, 'He let her go, watching her muslin figure under a parasol recede down the long colonnade of cob-nuts.' Of course, Miles follows her. The garden was erotically animated for Vita by the many sexual encounters with different women which she engineered there. These culminated at the Lake, or in the hayricks in the fields, or in her room in the tower. Vita replayed them all in her novels and poems, with herself cast as the man (her pet names in these relationships – 'David', for example, or 'Julian' – were invariably male).

At some stage in the mid 1930s Vita hit upon the idea of a 'Persian carpet', as she called it, of primroses and polyanthus in many colours, planted in the rough grass beneath the hazels, and flowering 'from early

RIGHT: The woodland understorey includes ferns, such as Onoclea sensibilis *(left), while* Maianthemum stellatum *– with yellow foliage – must be carefully managed to limit its spread.*

ABOVE: Woodland scenes: a carpet of Smyrnium perfoliatum *(top),* Trillium sessile *(above left)
and the white-flowered species,* T. grandiflorum *(above right).*

April till the second week in May in the broken light and shade of the Nuts'. These old florists' flowers had romantic appeal for Vita because of their undeniably antique flavour and 'quaintness', while their considerable horticultural appeal lay in the sheer range of varieties still available, in all kinds of colours and with thrilling (for the polyanthophile) variations in petal shapes. This was one of the few features at Sissinghurst which might be said to have been inspired directly by Gertrude Jekyll, whom Vita had visited with her mother in 1917 at Munstead Wood. There, the great gardener had made a primrose garden of multicoloured polyanthus flowers, shaded by a nut walk. Vita did not visit at the correct season to see them in flower, but she would have been aware of the idea. They were certainly in vogue again in the 1930s, when Vita found herself in the vanguard of fashion; a few years on, in 1939, Sacheverell Sitwell would produce a generous and detailed chapter on the topic in his *Old Fashioned Flowers*. The polyanthus carpet in the Nuttery became one of the most celebrated features of Sissinghurst. It was a surprising and jubilant display of optimism in this richly shadowed realm. Along with the White Garden and the Rose Garden, the polyanthus display was one of the main reasons to come to Sissinghurst in the 1950s.

Disaster finally struck in 1960, when the polyanthus began to sicken and die, affected by disease in the soil. The plant collection staggered on until 1974, when the Trust made the difficult decision to stop growing them altogether. Subsequently, the Nuttery has had to become something else. The display is not quite as startlingly colourful, but it does last rather longer – a good policy for a visitor attraction (though not, it must be admitted, a particular bonus in Vita's book). The tone at all seasons is now quiet and woodlandy, though it has its moments, such as early spring, when the ferns are at their freshest – notably *Matteuccia struthiopteris* (shuttlecock fern), *Onoclea sensibilis* (sensitive fern), *Adiantum aleuticum* 'Japonicum' and *Polystichum setiferum* 'Pulcherrimum Bevis'. Other plants to pique the interest include the black false hellebore (*Veratrum nigrum*), with thrusting purple spires; yellow-flowered *Allium moly*; and the characterful little *Anemone narcissiflora*. Lower down are the starry flowers of false Solomon's seal (*Maianthemum stellatum*). The chosen hardy geranium is *Geranium sylvaticum*, both 'Album' and 'Mayflower'. Ground-covering woodland plants include *Podophyllum peltatum*, *Tiarella cordifolia*, *Trillium grandiflorum* and *Uvularia perfoliata*, this last with impossibly elegant, drooping, pale yellow flowers. Epimediums are also prominent in the understorey, along with *Smyrnium perfoliatum*, a spreading plant with the acid-green colouration of a euphorbia flower. Towering above are white foxgloves, with *Euphorbia amygdaloides* var. *robbiae* creating a formal contrast alongside the hazels, now that all other shrubs, including *Euonymus alatus* and cornus, have been removed for reasons of simplicity and clarity.

The hazels themselves are now managed more as ornamental subjects than as true coppices, with fewer stems (up to twelve per plant), which are left to grow older and larger to enhance the impression of age. A few bulbous plants pop up: sprinklings of martagon lilies and the white form of the Spanish bluebell (the blue Spanish types are banished). Care is taken not to reprise any of the plantings already seen in the Spring Garden. Finally, several zingy or variegated grasses have been selected to light up ground level: yellow-green *Milium effusum* 'Aureum' and *Luzula sylvatica* 'Marginata', its leaves delicately margined with cream.

In truth, this remains, in essence, a highly seasonal garden – in the Sissinghurst tradition. The Nuttery is lit up with flowers and fresh green foliage from spring to early summer. But by early July, it is finished.

Standing in the middle of the Nuttery on a column base, and framed by the encroaching branches of the hazels, is a statue of a male bacchanalian figure to match the female one at the top of the Lime Walk. Young and handsome, with whorls of hair curled tightly on his head, this figure has something of Antinous about him, notwithstanding the wine cup in his hand. Such a reference would certainly have appealed to Harold, as Antinous was the Roman Emperor Hadrian's young lover, who in death became an enduring emblem of homosexuality. (The statue by the Moat can also be linked to Antinous in the same way, because in the classical era the deified Antinous was frequently presented as Dionysus.) Here, the statue enhances the mysterious character of the dappled woodland.

The Nuttery sits on the southern edge of the garden. In a controversial move, former head gardener Troy Scott Smith opened up this southern boundary by removing a 2.5-metre/8-foot-high clipped hornbeam hedge which used to constitute a definitive formal barrier between the garden and the adjacent fields. The idea was to break down that division, enabling 'a dialogue with countryside', while also allowing more light into this side of the Nuttery, so that informal plantings of phlomis, achillea and other border perennials could be tried.

The hornbeam itself has been replaced by a typical farm hedge of mainly hawthorn, kept low and quite raggedly cut. There is an exit from the garden into the fields halfway down the Lime Walk, and another at its eastern end – potentially quite an abrupt transition which is now being softened by the policy of treating the fields more as pasture. The intention is to encourage people to stray out of the garden proper, and to wander into the fields and, perhaps, down the slope towards the Lake, where a new gate is being installed. After all, the distance from the Spring Garden and Lime Walk to the Lake is about the same as it is to the White Garden. It just seems farther.

Ultimately, the great contribution of the Nuttery to Sissinghurst is that special quality of light. It brings to mind the other light effects offered up by the garden, which is perhaps unusually varied in this respect. Such qualities are derived from the presence of the high brick walls, the tower itself and all those thrusting roses and tumbling climbers. The cumulative impact of these physical features makes Sissinghurst a garden where light and shadow make a distinctively powerful contribution, whether that be because of shadows (near the tower and around the quartets of yews, for example); in the sheen of colours made by a canopy (as in the Nuttery); or as a result of the strong colouration of plant groupings (in the White Garden and the Rose Garden particularly). Sissinghurst is a garden which has a tendency to creep up and surprise the visitor, and very often a change in the quality of light is the reason. 🌱

RIGHT: Delicate accents: English bluebells (top left); epimedium foliage (top right); white Spanish bluebells with shuttlecock ferns (middle left); blue Omphalodes cappadocica *with white* Galium odoratum *(bottom left); and massed scillas (bottom right).*

INTERLUDE

A literary garden

'These fragments I have shored against my ruins'

❧ *The Waste Land* by T.S. Eliot, 1922

THE GARDEN AT SISSINGHURST can be interpreted as an authentic expression of Vita and Harold's unconventional marriage – perhaps more so, even, than their two children were. But Sissinghurst was also a self-conscious artistic expression which should be understood in the intellectual and cultural context of the time. No garden can be considered an island (even one that has a moat).

What, then, of Vita and Harold's peculiar yet enduring union? The story of Vita's elopement with Violet Trefusis, the love of her early life, has been told often enough. Both were married and the escapade led to the tragi-comical caper of their husbands pursuing them to France in a two-seater light aeroplane, in an attempt to break up the liaison. By the mid 1920s this had all calmed down. Harold and Vita settled into an open marriage based on an understanding that they were free to love whom they wanted, as long as there was tenderness and understanding between them, and obviously as little public embarrassment as possible.

PREVIOUS PAGE: The Rose Garden, with pink Erysimum scoparium *and* Euphorbia characias subsp. wulfenii *in front, and berberis and* Clematis montana *beyond. LEFT: Blossom and long grass in the tranquil Orchard.*

They genuinely felt that their marriage was something which others could emulate, and even gave a joint talk on BBC radio about it, though obviously they did not mention the truth about their sexual orientation (then illegal of course, for Harold). Nor did the fact come up that Vita was at the time engaged in an affair with Hilda Matheson, the head of BBC 'talks', who had commissioned the pair to regale the nation on this topic.

The first point to make about Vita and Harold's relationship is that, as with all loving partnerships, any outsider cannot fully understand its nature – and nor, in fact, will those within it, either, which is often a source of inner strength. Harold reported that their short pre-marriage courtship had been conducted without a single kiss – which does not mean to say it did not have its own sort of intimacy, that it was not a kind of love affair. As Vita wrote to Harold much later, in 1926: 'the liaisons which you and I contract are something perfectly apart from the more natural and normal attitude we have towards each other, and therefore don't interfere.'

When Harold was posted to Tehran in the mid 1920s and Vita stayed on in England, they were left free to pursue various same-sex affairs and dalliances, both partners in the marriage in full knowledge of the fact.

Vita once wrote to Harold:

I was thinking 'How queer! I suppose Hadji [Harold] and I have been about as unfaithful to one another as one well could be from the conventional point of view, even worse than unfaithful if you add in homosexuality, and yet I swear no two people could love one another more than we do after all these years.' It is queer, isn't it? It does destroy all orthodox ideas of marriage?

It is interesting that Vita uses the term 'destroy' here. It is a violent way of making the point. In some ways Sissinghurst was a retreat into the privacy they required. They felt they had to hide away the unorthodox nature of their marriage because of society and the law, and played a game of half-denying their homosexuality to each other. But in other ways it was a dynamic and expressive confirmation of the validity of their own way of living together: 'A Marriage of One's Own'. The strange success of their marriage destroys the superstructure of traditional wedlock, just as the garden's layout in some sense shatters any expectations derived from the Arts and Crafts tradition, in which the garden supposedly sits. As another great garden-maker and poet Ian Hamilton Finlay later put it: 'Certain gardens are described as retreats when they are really attacks.' Sissinghurst's garden reflects the complexities of Vita and Harold's partnership – and is also a form of confrontation. Privately, and in their own way, by making the garden, they were standing firm against the expectations of the world outside. At Sissinghurst they were fashioning 'another world than this' (the title of the anthology they edited together).

Their garden was a place for emotional healing, too. In a poem that Vita wrote to Harold in 1937, she states 'let us cram with flowers each threatened rift'. This is an alternative way of understanding Vita's 'cram, cram, cram'. The psychological and the horticultural collide,

combine and are resolved – any cracks in their marriage will be filled with flowers.

Since Eden, the garden has been a zone of both liberation and transgression in human affairs, and Sissinghurst also gave Vita and Harold the freedom to express their true selves. Harold, through the statues of handsome young men and experimentation with colour in the Spring Garden; Vita, through an 'exotic' repertoire of flowers that assimilated her own 'foreignness'. There were many other ways they expressed themselves in the garden. Indeed, for Vita especially, it meant playing apparently contradictory roles in this dramatic arena: masculine and feminine, English and Spanish, expert and amateur, sensualist and technician, mother and lover, poet and gardener, chaste mystic and seducer, wife and mistress, gypsy and aristocrat, chatelaine and recluse.

The broken mirror
The garden at Sissinghurst was always going to be a frustrated or shattered dream, a mirror of the world that is distorted or fragmentary. The kaleidoscopic shards of that broken mirror lend it an emotional intensity which continues to draw us in.

Vita used the mirror analogy several times, as we will see later in the context of the Lake and its trees. The garden can be understood as a physical and metaphorical re-enactment of these broken shards of Vita's (and, to an extent, Harold's) different identities. The facets or fragments of the garden – what Harold called 'a succession of privacies' – are engineered to express themselves at different times of year, and have quite distinct personalities, akin to the different roles Vita played in public and private. The expression of these competing identities through the spaces of the garden was a source of intense solace and pleasure to Vita; it

RIGHT: The White Garden, with Rosa *'Mulliganii' on the arbour, the plumes of* Aruncus dioicus *'Kneiffii' (left) and the tower looming above.*

own in the garden, when all these competing identities can be reconciled in privacy and played out.

Harold picked up on Vita's apparent contradictions, at one point complaining: 'But what has always worried me is your dual personality. The one tender, wise and with such a sense of responsibility. And the other rather cruel and extravagant.' In truth he is writing here about the side of Vita which loves him, and the side that has multiple affairs with women.

Even the clothes Vita wore for gardening were a sort of costume which allowed her to be her true self through role playing. In her confessional memoir, written in 1920 at the age of 28 and later published by Nigel Nicolson as *Portrait of a Marriage*, Vita recounted the moment of epiphany she had experienced two years before with Violet Trefusis during her stay at Long Barn, while Harold was away.

> *...everything changed suddenly — changed far more than I foresaw at the time; changed my life. It was the 18th of April. An absurd circumstance gave rise to the whole thing; I had just got clothes like the women-on-the-land were wearing, and in the unaccustomed freedom of breeches and gaiters I went into wild spirits; I ran, I shouted, I jumped, I climbed, I vaulted over gates, I felt like a schoolboy let out on a holiday; and Violet followed me across fields and woods with a new meekness, saying very little, but never taking her eyes off me...I remember that wild irresponsible day. It was one of the most vibrant days of my life.*

truly was a parallel world in which she could happily exist, orchestrating the garden's effects as a commentary on the varying textures of her own emotional life. In one poem, Vita bemoans the effect of visitors upon her, recalling instead those times:

> *When no one comes to take me away from myself*
> *And turn me into a patchwork, a jig-saw puzzle,*
> *A broken mirror that once gave a whole reflection,*
> *Being so contrived that it takes too long a time*
> *To get myself back to myself when they have gone.*

Vita feels that outsiders force her to perform one particular role, as opposed to the time she spends on her

Vita considered herself to be bisexual, though in the event, all of her relationships from the 1920s onwards were with women. Her head had first been turned in this direction — or rather, she was made aware of these

ABOVE: The view from the Cottage Garden down the Moat Walk towards the Dionysus statue, with white wisteria foaming over the wall.

feelings – by Princess Marie (later Queen of Romania), no less, a famous beauty and granddaughter of Queen Victoria, who lived in Kent during Vita's childhood. She visited Knole, where Vita was captivated by her glamorous, regal charisma: she 'set my feet along the wrong path', as she revealed in passing, much later on.

The 'wrong' path? Socially conservative, Vita often made comments such as this about her own sexual preferences, sometimes referring to herself as an aberration or even as perverted, though on other occasions she could be delicate and perceptive about her 'dual nature'. Understandably, given the milieu into which she was born, she struggled to escape from the cultural expectations bulwarked around marriage, and sometimes thought of herself as a failure in that sense. She did use the word 'lesbian' in some letters to Harold and others, but earlier on the term 'Sapphic' (referring to the Ancient Greek female poet Sappho) was preferred. It sounds a little coy, perhaps, today, but at that point it was simply the most used word for a sexual orientation which Queen Victoria reputedly refused to believe existed in reality, a position echoed in Vita's own lifetime by (of all people) her lover Virginia Woolf's mother-in-law.

There is no doubt that Vita was a highly sexed individual. Woolf chided her for her promiscuity, and with some justification, from her point of view, because it is true that Vita pursued anyone who took her fancy at any given moment, regardless of whether she was engaged in any other potentially more serious relationship. With Vita, it was not so much a matter of love triangles as love dodecahedrons. In one of her poems she referred to these predatory affairs with women as 'cheap and easy loves', though the other half in the relationship was not always as cavalier about it. As one of her frustrated paramours wrote to her: 'But you do like to have your cake and eat it, – and so many cakes, so many, a surfeit of sweet things.' She led on her girlfriends, and sometimes also sought to justify a new relationship to Harold by framing

it all in intensely romantic terminology – when in reality these were often lusty liaisons founded chiefly or only on sexual attraction. (Woolf, for one, was dismayed by this non-intellectual aspect of Vita's love life during the period of their intimacy – it upset her more than the infidelity itself.)

Vita seemed to inspire extreme reactions in people, especially women, who sometimes found themselves unexpectedly and transgressively drawn to her. On one occasion in Cincinnati, during a lecture tour in 1933, Vita recorded in her diary: 'A lady comes up afterwards, and tells me she has had a vision during my lecture, and that I was Balkis, Queen of Sheba, in a previous incarnation. Try to look suitably grateful.' Several marriages were destroyed as a result of this obsession with the elegant aristocratic lady from the Kentish castle, clad in her battle dress of pearls, silk blouse, riding breeches and lace-up leather boots, cigarette-holder poised in hand. There was almost something of the dominatrix about her; there are intimations in letters and poetry that she was a passionate lover to the point of violence, or at least the inflicting of pain.

Fortunately, it seems Harold was not fazed by Vita and all those competing female Vs dominating her life. Victoria, her overbearing mother. Violet, her great romantic love. Virginia, her great intellectual love. And, of course, Vita herself at the centre.

As for Harold, his encounters with men – all conducted 'in town' (London), never at Sissinghurst, as far as we know – were much more fleeting; none of them could be described as anything like a love affair. His son Nigel Nicolson stated, in his portion of *Portrait of a Marriage*: 'Harold had a series of relationships with men who were his intellectual equals, but the physical element in them was very secondary. He was never a passionate lover. To him sex was as incidental, and about as pleasurable, as a quick visit to a picture-gallery between trains.' There may be some truth in this, but it also rather smacks of the highly conservative son attempting to water down or 'excuse' his father's homosexuality – to the point where it barely exists.

One way of gaining a more precise understanding of Vita and Harold's relationship is through *Another World Than This*, the anthology of verse they published as joint editors in 1945. The choices they made for this unaccountably overlooked volume (the only book they ever produced together) constitute a kind of code that unlocks their marriage. The contract made between them is reflected in a quotation from the 1st century BC Latin poet Tibullus, which they translate as:

(It is lust) that guides the girl who creeps alone to her lover in the night. Slyly she steps over the prone bodies of her guardians; holding her breath in suspense, she feels with her feet the path that stretches before her, and with hand held in front of her she feels her way along the passage in the dark.

Both Vita and Harold did a fair amount of stumbling along passages in the dark in unfamiliar houses. These lines are essentially a celebration and validation of their open marriage.

Their project at Sissinghurst is triumphantly asserted in a line from the *Lysis*, Plato's dialogue on the different sorts of friendship, which they translate as: 'For I assert that the good is beautiful, don't you agree? Of course I do.' This sums up their creed; for Harold and Vita, the beautiful thing they had made, Sissinghurst's garden, was an inalienable good and the chief justification of their lives together.

And a line from Virgil's *Georgics* (that great pastoral poem which was so important to Vita) expresses their simple, unalloyed joy at working together on the garden: 'Such is their love of flowers and the glory which they find in building honey.' There is much more of this to explore in the anthology, including the passage from Homer which stands as the epigraph for the Introduction to this book.

Vita and Virginia

Vita's partnership with Harold represented only one aspect of her emotional and intellectual life. Almost as important was her relationship with Virginia Woolf. It could even be argued that certain aspects of the novelist's experimental literary style percolated into the structure and tone of Vita's garden.

Vita met Virginia at a Bloomsbury dinner party given in 1922 by Clive Bell, who was at that point Vita's only connection with the group. The two women were immediately drawn to each other's company and soon in love. The meaning of their relationship was mainly bound up in their conversations and intimacies concerning literature and art. This does not mean to imply that it was not a romantic and sexual relationship. It was – chiefly in the period 1925–28. But theirs was a love founded mainly on awestruck mutual fascination, shared ambitions and a deep admiration, verging on adulation, on both sides. They were intimate friends for a long time after the early period of their ardour – until something of a break finally occurred in 1935.

The idea of a garden as a zone of eroticism became a theme for them. In the first flush of their relationship, while Vita was staying with her, Virginia wrote to her sister Vanessa Bell and described her own garden as 'full of lust and bees'. Reminiscent of this is a passage from Woolf's 1939 essay 'A Sketch of the Past':

The gardens gave off a murmur of bees; the apples were red and gold; there were also pink flowers; and grey and silver leaves. The buzz, the croon, the smell, all seemed to press voluptuously against some membrane; not to burst it; but to hum round one such a complete rapture of pleasure that I stopped, smelt; looked.

Virginia was drawn to Vita partly because as an aristocrat she was, in a way, a historical artefact. In 1927 she went to visit Knole with Vita and described the experience in her diary: 'All the centuries seemed lit up, the past expressive, articulate; not dumb & forgotten; but a crowd of people stood behind, not dead at all; not remarkable; fair faced, long limbed; affable; & so we reach the days of Elizabeth quite easily.'

Vita was like a ghost from the past to Virginia – who played a game of flirtatiously addressing her as 'my lady' in her letters, in cod-Shakespearean vein. As it happened, Vita also saw herself in this way, as a character somehow caught out of time. Such seductive ideas eventually coalesced in Virginia's love letter to Vita, the novel *Orlando* (1928), conceived in homage to the exiled would-

be chatelaine of Knole. Harold had already experimented with these ideas in his semi-fictional memoir *Some People* (1927), which Virginia had reviewed favourably.

Perhaps it sounds a tall order to detect meaningful comparisons between two genres – literature and garden-making – which outwardly appear to have little in common. But the same minds, Harold's and Vita's, were intensively at work on both these matters, at the same time and over many years, so perhaps a sense of kinship, or even creative parallels, may be teased out.

For the Bloomsbury group, with whom Vita was loosely associated through her friendship with the Woolfs,

ABOVE: Looking back across the wintry eastern fields dusted with frost towards Sissinghurst and its fairy-tale tower.

the domestic milieu emerged as a key preoccupation, at places such as Charleston, in Sussex, where the decoration of house and, to some extent, garden was a communal effort. The house described in *Howards End* (1910), a novel by E.M. Forster, a key figure in the Bloomsbury group, has been described as a domestic utopia whose occupants were able to achieve intellectual fulfilment and (implied) sexual emancipation. Arguably, this was the kind of liberated atmosphere Vita and Harold were aiming for at Sissinghurst, where the 'rooms' of the garden they made transcend all domestic expectations, truly creating 'another world than this'.

Sissinghurst: the modernist garden

The kind of modernism (and there are many modernisms) being essayed by the Bloomsbury group was far more individualistic and libertarian in essence than the brave new worlds envisaged by architectural modernists like Le Corbusier, whose attitudes tended to be egalitarian, if not socialistic. Nor is Sissinghurst a modernist garden

in the landscape-architectural sense, as it was being espoused at this time by theorists such as Christopher Tunnard, whose various magazine articles were revised and collected as *Gardens in the Modern Landscape* (1938). The modernism that was an influence on Vita and Harold was literary modernism – which is perhaps understandable, since they were both primarily literary people (and described themselves as such). Arguably, those ideas were then transmuted into physical form in the garden, affecting its structure, progression and overall tone.

'Stream-of-consciousness' is a technique associated with literary modernism and particularly Woolf: the articulation of the thought processes of a character, seemingly as they might occur in life, allowing the reader access, apparently, to their innermost fears and desires. An argument can be made that Sissinghurst was

ABOVE: The northern branch of the Moat at first light, with the gazebo at the north-east corner of the Orchard.

in part inspired by stream-of-consciousness and other experimental techniques that Woolf employed in novels such as *To the Lighthouse* (1927) and *The Waves* (1931), which were written in the period of Vita and Virginia's intimacy. The psychologist-philosopher William James, who coined the term in 1890, used the image of a river to describe 'the stream of thought, of consciousness, or of subjective life', but it might be contended that the ever-changing garden, equally, is a fit metaphor for this description of consciousness as it is lived. In *To the Lighthouse*, Mrs Ramsay turns to the natural world for a sense of identification: 'It was odd, she thought, how if one was alone, one leant to things, inanimate things; trees, streams, flowers; felt they expressed one; felt they became one; felt they knew one, in a sense were one.'

Perhaps this can be applied directly to Vita and Sissinghurst? Her garden was ultimately indivisible from her self. And the texture of Harold's garden layout could be described as 'stream-of-consciousness' in effect, it is so unbridled, instinctive and easy-flowing. Harold's overall design has the virtue of appearing spontaneous, even while it is underpinned by problem-solving geometric organisation. The reason it seems logical to visitors is because it develops in a way that feels natural to the human mind and body when walking the garden at ground level. On paper, of course, it appears to be disastrous, yet it speaks to us more deeply than a rational ground plan ever could.

Woolf's novel *Mrs Dalloway* (1925) is generally held to be her first important foray into the technique of stream-of-consciousness, and it is noteworthy that at around the same time Vita published her most experimental novel by far, *Seducers in Ecuador* (1924). The *Spectator* described the book as 'a slim, fantastic conte in the best Bloomsbury manner', and it was commercially successful (outselling *Mrs Dalloway*). But its style comes across as glibly fashionable; Vita's own disappointment with it led to a six-year period during which she wrote

no fiction – until the publication of the much more conventional and bestselling *The Edwardians* saved Vita and Harold, financially, just as they arrived at Sissinghurst. Outwardly, Vita may have decried literary modernism, even telling some friends that *Seducers in Ecuador* was a joke, but it is clear that in some ways she was desperate to write in a more contemporary manner, to 'keep up' with the likes of Woolf, James Joyce and D.H. Lawrence. Later, in a letter to an American writer acquaintance, she confessed: 'You ask which of my novels I prefer. I dislike them all, – *Seducers in Ecuador* is the only one I might save from the rubbish-heap.'

Vita tried one more time to produce experimental, modernist fiction – with marginally more success. The topic of *All Passion Spent* (1931) is the emancipation of an elderly lady, and a meditation on impending death. The themes are interesting but again it is stylistically unconvincing: Vita essays a watered-down form of stream-of-consciousness in this novel, and ultimately the result is a Woolworths version of *Mrs Dalloway*.

Perhaps her most successful foray into literary modernism was not in fiction but poetry. Vita's long poem *Solitude* (1938) is modernist and experimental in structure, if not always in expression, with stanzas of unequal length and the abandonment of any formal rhyme scheme. Like all of Vita's long-form poetry, *Solitude* is decidedly uneven in quality, but its meditative, almost prayerful tone and candour prove to be a relief in the context of her rather over-mannered style elsewhere.

These attempts by Vita to create a work of fiction worthy of her admired lover Virginia (*Seducers in Ecuador* was dedicated to her) prove that she was open to these literary effects. There is no reason to suppose that she was not equally open to the idea of making a garden that was as sophisticated in psychological terms, as opposed to the mere piece of romanticised escapism which is usually described. Vita wanted above all to be a great writer; in truth, she was a talented journalist, a mediocre though commercially successful novelist, a competent poet, and a garden-maker of historical importance.

There are other echoes of literary modernism in the garden. W.B. Yeats's celebrated line, so evocative of the crisis of spiritual confidence of the first decades of the 20th century – 'Things fall apart; the centre cannot hold' – comes to mind at several points at Sissinghurst, perhaps most intensely in the Tower Lawn, which stands as a nexus of uncertainty in the middle of the garden. Arguably, the structure of Sissinghurst also betrays the influence of T.S. Eliot, whose great poem *The Waste Land* (1922) was in part the inspiration for Vita's own *The Land* (1926). To her friends, Vita excoriated what she called the 'dunghill despair' of Eliot's vision, returning to the theme years later in her poem *The Garden* (1946), in which she quoted the first four lines of *The Waste Land* ('April is the cruellest month…'), producing this riposte:

> *The land and not the waste land celebrate,*
> *The rich and hopeful land, the solvent land*

Yet Vita was obviously affected enough by Eliot's poem to want to produce a response – which in a literary context is most certainly a compliment. In fact, she and Harold had great admiration for 'Tom' Eliot, who was a well-liked satellite member of the Bloomsbury group. Harold attended at least one lecture by Eliot and was dazzled by his erudition and easy style. Eliot's conservative, latterly religious outlook, as well as the conventional humility of his day job in a bank, also appealed to Vita and Harold in a way that the work and style of younger, left-wing tyros, such as W.H. Auden, did not. Vita quoted twelve lines – those 'fine lines' – from *The Waste Land* in her lecture 'Some Tendencies of Modern English Poetry' (1928) and ended it with a quotation from Eliot's poem 'The Hollow Men', though she had her reservations about contemporary poetry: 'they reject the old, quite rightly, and we, quite rightly, are dissatisfied with the new.'

With her instinctively patrician sensibility, Vita was uncomfortable with a literature that reflected society's directionless alienation. It was her role, as an aristocrat, to provide a sense of purpose.

Nevertheless, a different strain, a romantic, pastoral sort of feeling, did emerge in several late-modernist texts, including Forster's 'pageant-play' novel, *England's Pleasant Land* (1940), and even Eliot's own *Four Quartets* (1943). One of the most piquant expressions of this was Woolf's novel *Between the Acts* (1941), which is also framed around the device of a pageant play, a 'historical' community performance, of a kind that was popular at country houses in the 1920s and 1930s. Woolf uses techniques of fragmentation, quotation and close observation to commentate on the disintegration of a traditional English way of life, while also acknowledging its strengths. In a way, the 'hero' of the book is Pointz Hall, an old house which is much loved and will endure despite social change. There are key moments throughout the novel when the house, its garden and even the weather seem to reflect the general current of British culture (and obviously the war in Europe). During the performance itself, which takes up most of the book, everything stops:

> *And then the shower fell, sudden, profuse. No one had seen the cloud coming. There it was, black, swollen, on top of them. Down it poured like all the people in the world weeping…The rain was sudden and universal. Then it stopped. From the grass rose a fresh earthy smell.*

Woolf seemed to catch another aspect of this in a stray sentence in her essay 'Evening Over Sussex: Reflections in a Motor Car', written in around 1927: 'Also the fields are redeemed.' The Kent landscape had a redemptive

RIGHT: Snake's head fritillaries and narcissus flowering in the rough grass beneath the trees in the Orchard.

quality for Vita, certainly – that is the overwhelming sentiment of her poem *The Land*. The garden became a kind of redemption, too, over time. The climax of a modernist text is often a moment of epiphany, a sudden realisation of absolute truth (the most celebrated instance of this occurs in *To the Lighthouse*). A sense of (secular) redemption is often bound up with this. And what is a garden if not a succession of epiphanies which constantly remake themselves every day of the year? The garden at Sissinghurst was a source of profound epiphanic solace for Vita and Harold – as gardens have proven to be for so many people.

This was an elegiac modernism, then, looking back intensely even as it supposedly looked forward. (And there is something very English about this paradox, which is rooted in the national obsession with the pastoral.) As such, it was more suited to Vita's purposes. Throughout her literary career – or at least after she had met Virginia Woolf – Vita was torn between her natural inclination to write traditional verse on chiefly pastoral themes, and an urge to experiment in a more modernist-inflected milieu. The garden at Sissinghurst displays a similar dichotomy of aspiration, being in some ways deeply traditional – all those roses, the orchard trees – while in other ways it rips up the rule book of garden design – the deconstructed layout, the incongruous frissons of the exotic.

That hybrid position between the psychological sophistication of modernism and the romantic English pastoral tradition was something that defined the mid-century period in intellectual Britain (and arguably continues to do so). Vita may not have wished to subscribe to the superficially nihilistic view of the modern world espoused by Eliot in *The Waste Land*, but potentially something of its fragmentary structure can be found echoed in the garden at Sissinghurst. 'These fragments

I have shored against my ruins', wrote Eliot (half-quoting Isaiah) in the final lines of the poem, and this might stand as an alternative epigraph for Vita and Harold's garden – which was, after all, described in the estate agent's particulars as 'picturesque ruins in grounds'. When they arrived, the putative garden at Sissinghurst was very nearly their last stand: Harold had no job and was low on cash, while Vita was coming to terms with the end of her relationship with Virginia, and gradually withdrawing from the world. They were also faced with the ongoing challenge of their unorthodox marriage, the survival of which must have felt like a miracle at times. Those fragments truly were being shored.

These are the concluding lines of *The Waste Land*:

> I sat upon the shore
> Fishing, with the arid plain behind me
> Shall I at least set my lands in order?
> London Bridge is falling down falling down falling down
> *Poi s'ascose nel foco che gli affina*
> *Quando fiam uti chelidon* – O swallow swallow
> *Le Prince d'Aquitaine à la tour abolie*
> These fragments I have shored against my ruins
> Why then Ile fit you. Hieronymo's mad againe.
> Datta. Dayadhvam. Damyata.
> Shantih shantih shantih

Eliot's poem was published by Leonard and Virginia Woolf's Hogarth Press, as were Vita's books (indeed, her bestselling novels helped bankroll more experimental work – including Woolf's own output). Despite Vita's misgivings about the poem, certain similarities can be found between *The Waste Land* and Sissinghurst. Both deal in fragments and quotations, sometimes put together in jarring, staccato juxtaposition. A sense of disorientation is a recurring motif. They both rely on a dazzling and sometimes mystifying array of effects (poetic and horticultural) drawn from every corner of the world,

which come together in a kind of slow-motion explosion. In each there are snatches of the English vernacular, classical myth, the 'antique' 17th century, modernity and a frisson of the East. Both poem and garden speak to us in various languages (all those old roses with French names, all that Latin taxonomy), and both ultimately work upon us as reflections of the complexity of social and emotional life in the 20th century. We move through the poem and the garden as if in a dream. Finally Eliot turns to the physical landscape as a source of possible redemption, from the disaster of 'London Bridge is falling down' to the declarative 'Shall I at least set my lands in order?' A garden is nothing else if not an act of creative defiance in the face of the destructive chaos of nature. Eliot's lines in Italian and French are also defiant and optimistic in tone: Dante's '*Poi s'ascose nel foco che gli affina*' means 'And then he hid in the fire that refines them.' This suggests that one can take refuge in the midst of that which might be the destruction of us. Harold and Vita always knew that Sissinghurst was a risk – but that the prize was great. Then there is the line taken from a sonnet by the French poet Gérard de Nerval: '*Le Prince d'Aquitaine à la tour abolie*'. It translates as: 'The Prince of Aquitaine in the ruined tower'. Which needs no gloss here.

Finally, we must return to what is arguably the key line of the poem: 'These fragments I have shored against my ruins'. For T.S. Eliot and Vita Sackville-West alike, an aesthetic of fragmentation and hybridisation was the only possible response to 20th-century culture. For both, a policy of retreat – towards God, for the one, into a garden, for the other – was the only way to go forward, the only way to carry on. 🦋

RIGHT: The Cottage Garden at dawn, with the tall spikes of the orangey foxglove Digitalis ferruginea *vying for dominance with the yew topiaries.*

CHAPTER SIX

HERB GARDEN AND THYME LAWN

'Sweet Thyme, that underfoot so meekly grows
In humble company
Of splendid rose,
Is satisfied to be
The acolyte, each gardener knows,
Of lavender, of rue, and rosemary.'

❧ 'Sweet Time' by Vita Sackville-West, 1921

THE HERB GARDEN is one of Sissinghurst's great surprises. The far corner of a garden is not the place you would expect to find such a diminutive, domesticated, hedged-in space for culinary plants. It is an incongruous moment of formality at the garden's edge, just where it meets the wider landscape. Here, the professionals' convention, learned since the era of Humphry Repton, the Regency landscape designer, would normally hold: farther away from the house, it is better to allow formality to dissolve. But, of course, this is Sissinghurst, where practicality, professionalism and normality were never high on the agenda. Vita and Harold were engaged in erecting a bulwark of dreams and beautiful moments to set against the lowering depredations of the world outside.

The truth is, Vita and Harold did not quite know what to do with this yew enclosure when they planted the hedges in 1934. It started as a cherry orchard, only becoming the Herb Garden in 1938, and in the event it

PREVIOUS PAGE: White achillea dominates this part of the garden, with blue chicory and a hop growing on a pole behind, while evening primrose appears to the right. LEFT: Artemisia pontica (left) and Filipendula ulmaria (right) flank the central path, leading to a simple wooden seat.

was to be chiefly an ornamental and historical display. Vita also used its produce as ingredients for the Knole potpourri, a scent that had suffused her childhood and which she religiously recreated every year. She described the recipe in her book on Knole. It begins: 'Gather dry, Double Violets, Rose Leaves, Lavender, Myrtle flowers, Verbena, Bay leaves, Rosemary, Balm, Musk, Geranium [pelargonium]. Pick these from the stalks and dry on paper in the sun for a day or two before putting them in a jar.' The herbs in this herb garden were not being grown to be eaten. The plot was situated about as far away as it is possible to be from the kitchen, which was located in the Priest's House (where a small 'real' herb garden had been made, in what is now the White Garden). For Vita was not interested in cookery and never wrote about it. She employed a daily cook and did not interfere.

It was not Vita but her gardener, Jack Vass, who took it upon himself to reinvigorate the Herb Garden after the war. By 1948 he was growing around sixty varieties in there. Perhaps Vita looked upon this area as essentially the servants' realm. (A chamomile seat made here was apparently the creation of Vita and Harold's chauffeur.) Either way, there has always been something a little bit fake, perhaps even a tiny bit 'Marie Antoinette', about this part of the garden. As a surprising little episode, the Herb Garden adds a certain quirkiness and a moment of abrupt disorientation after the cool 'non-design' of the Nuttery. Perhaps its most curious physical aspect is the highly decorative quality of the surrounding yew hedge, which is clipped into rather grand buttresses of the kind you would expect to see at a more conventional Arts and Crafts garden — along the back of a long double border, for example, forming compartments.

If this incongruously grandiose Herb Garden was conceived as a joke, a juxtaposition of the ultra-formal with the everyday, then it is a joke of the same species of mock-heroic used in the deliberately suburban naming of Sissinghurst Crescent, the box exedra and seat at the head of the Moat Walk. The mock-heroic was a literary tone with which Harold and Vita would have been familiar, through the work of 18th-century poets such as Alexander Pope. Such jokes were intended to undercut any potential accusations of pomposity or pretension on the part of the garden's creators; that was a trap which Vita and Harold went to great lengths to avoid.

The characterful stone bowl on lion supports at the centre of the garden, in which succulents are grown, serves as a reminder of the first, necessarily short-lived garden the newly-weds made together in Constantinople, where Harold had been posted as a diplomat in 1912, before Vita's pregnancy (and the First World War) interrupted. That is where they had originally installed this singular accoutrement. The fancy sunburst design made of tiles laid on edge around the central bowl was an addition of Nigel Nicolson's in 1970 and does not quite seem to fit in. It formalises the space further, when the original intention was for it all to be rather tumbledown

RIGHT: The bowl on lion supports — brought back from Constantinople by Vita and Harold — contains Jovibarba *succulents.*

Today, the quartet of beds around the Herb Garden's low central bowl bubbles away with a mix of the familiar – thymes, hyssops, tansies, coriander, alliums – and the slightly more esoteric, such as *Artemisia pontica* (Roman wormwood, used for absinthe), poisonous *Aristolochia clematitis* (birthwort), medicinal *Arnica montana* and *Lablab purpureus*, the hyacinth bean, with vivid pinkish-purple pods. Other specimens of interest to be discovered ranged around the more common herbs, such as sorrel, mint and lovage, are *Glycyrrhiza glabra* (liquorice), *Isatis tinctoria* (woad), *Hyoscyamus niger* (henbane), *Monarda citriodora* (lemon bee balm) and purple-flowered *Nicandra physalodes* (shoo-fly plant). It has to be said that very few of these more unusual plants were grown here in Vita's day. She rarely grew anything for its botanical interest alone, unless it was a 'queer' plant which intrigued her. (There was a vogue for such curiosities: E.A. Bowles of Myddelton House, whose books Vita owned, had a patch of curious or contorted plants in his garden which he named 'the lunatic asylum'.) For Vita, all that mattered was that a plant had to look 'right' *in situ*, in the Robinsonian tradition. Set against the east hedge are a few roses – such as *Rosa damascena* 'Professeur Émile Perrot' – while teasels (*Dipsacus fullonum*, the native species) add a note of wildness in the north-east corner.

Immediately to the north of the Herb Garden, and associated with it, is the Thyme Lawn. This feature has undergone several incarnations over the years but Vita's original conception was discussed in her 'Country Notes' column in the *New Statesman and Nation* (as the magazine was then called) in 1938: 'There is one sort of garden which I much want to possess. It is an Alpine lawn.' She goes on to describe her ideal alpine lawn as composed

– verging on the overgrown, even – within those clipped-hedge walls. The proof of this intention can be seen in a photograph used to illustrate Vita's article in the RHS *Journal* in 1953, and presumably approved by her: in it, the Herb Garden is looking rather shaggy, the yew hedges somewhat tufty; decidedly unsmart.

At the same time as the tiling was introduced, the old concrete slabs were replaced with a smart (too smart?) cruciform system of York-stone paths, with brick side paths. The paving of the Herb Garden is one of those little details that the Trust introduced quite early on, ostensibly for practical reasons, but which almost imperceptibly yet decisively shifts the tone away from Vita and Harold's style.

ABOVE: Wild bergamot, a magnet for bees. RIGHT: Simple scented moments: coriander (top left); bupleurum (top right); Pelargonium fragrans *(middle left);* violet *(middle);* myrtle *(bottom left); and* lavender *(bottom right).*

of 'the densest and most creeping sort' of thyme, with gentians, scillas, grape hyacinths, mini narcissi, 'those very small Persian and Greek tulips' and four 'John Downie' crab apples at the corners.

In the event, Vita did not plant trees around her Thyme Lawn of two separate beds, though she did intermix with the thyme certain bulbous plants, such as crocus, cyclamen and small narcissi. The idea was for a Persian carpet effect, to continue the theme of both Harold's Unter den Linden plantings in the Spring Garden and the polyanthus and primrose carpet of the Nuttery. It was certainly an experimental planting – but that was the essence of Vita's gardening. She often planted up to a dozen species or varieties of a genus which had taken

her fancy in the nursery garden. She would look at which of them did well in the soil and then select one or two (sometimes none) that she felt might fit the desired tone.

The Thyme Lawn occupies a space at the southern end of the Moat where it abruptly ends, providing a link area between the Herb Garden and the Moat Walk, while also relating to the Nuttery, the Orchard and the Moat itself. Its delimited edges – for this is not a 'garden room' – is yet another one of those intuitive design decisions at Sissinghurst which is easy to take for granted but is

OPPOSITE: Tall yellow verbascums and fennel frame a thriving clump of white tansy. ABOVE: The chamomile seat was originally the contribution of Vita and Harold's chauffeur.

extremely clever on the ground. Vita generally took care not to boast, but she does appear to have been quite proud of pulling off the Thyme Lawn, horticulturally speaking, claiming the feature as her own invention. She described its composition briefly in the RHS *Journal* of 1953, adding that it was 'cheap and quick and easy to produce'. One regret was that she had included white varieties of thyme in her carpet, since when it was complete she felt that purples and mauves would have sufficed.

On the topic of Vita's journalistic writing, it is noteworthy that in her columns for the *Observer* (from 29 September 1946 to 26 February 1961) she essentially erases Sissinghurst by leaving it out of the discussion, even though it is the only garden she can possibly be writing about, especially as she became more reclusive from the 1950s. (In her lesser-known, pre-war columns for the *New Statesman and Nation* and other magazines, Vita is not so chary of talking about her own garden.) The result is that features such as the Thyme Lawn are made to sound quite generic and repeatable, when in reality her style was original to the point of idiosyncrasy.

The Thyme Lawn has recently been entirely revamped. The two raised beds were removed and a terrace of artfully antiquated and broken-up paving stones has been installed in place. The number of varieties has been rationalised down to three reliable performers: a red thyme, a white thyme and a taller variety have been planted in the crevices, together with pennyroyal mint as a fail-safe spreader. This is not entirely faithful to Vita's original horticultural prescription, but one of the problems before was that some thymes did not wish to grow here, since there is quite a lot of shade. The justification is that the end result will be closer to the effect she desired, which was of one continuous 'lawn'. A sophisticated system of soil and drainage has been introduced, as well as some irrigation during the period of establishment. A pair of Lutyens benches has been added against the Herb Garden hedge on the southern side, shaded by 'very casual' standard wisterias, with purple violets growing under the seats and a stand of bupleurum on the Nuttery side to create a feeling of privacy. It may transpire that two Lutyens seats in a row prove to be too much of a good thing. Yet there is no doubt that the view north from here along the tree-shaded Moat is one of the most evocative in the whole of Sissinghurst. The atmosphere is transcendentally tranquil. 🦋

RIGHT: Vita used three kinds of thyme for her Thyme Lawn: a white, a pink and a dark pink variety.

CHAPTER SEVEN

THE MOAT
AND MOAT WALK

'I mean we have got what we wanted to get – a perfect proportion between the classic and the romantic, between the element of expectation and the element of surprise. Thus the main axes are terminated in a way to satisfy expectation, yet they are in themselves so tricky that they also cause surprise.'

❦ Letter from Harold Nicolson to Vita
Sackville-West, 8 June 1937

AT THE MOAT, Sissinghurst dissolves. 'I've sunk into an image, water-drowned', wrote Vita in her poem *Sissinghurst*. This is the end of the garden. Lethe, river of forgetfulness.

Within the boundaries described by the Moat, there is the garden – rich, characterful, imbued with human personality. Without, there is farmland and the gentle contours of the Wealden countryside: fields interrupted by parcels of oak and ash, old hedgerows and gates, rutted farm tracks, pockets of scrub and woodland that hide secret brooks and boggy patches.

The relationship between garden and countryside is stark, unmediated. The Moat is the garden's protective forcefield, Sissinghurst's defence, a means of blocking out encroachers and intruders. This is most intensely experienced at the far north-eastern corner of the garden, where the two branches of the Moat meet. Here there stands a little wooden summer house with a conical roof

that gives it something of the air of an oast house. This 'gazebo' was designed for Harold just before he died, a gift from his sons Nigel and Ben. The little hut is usually shut to visitors, but this corner of the garden is a good place from which to survey Sissinghurst's surroundings. Across the Moat to the north-east is an intersection of three farm tracks, with a barred gate into a field and hedgerows shooting off in different directions across the Faversham Weald. There is no road in sight but this is palpably a place of agricultural business, stretching as far as the eye can see 'under the pale wide heaven and slow clouds', as Vita described the Kentish countryside in her poem *The Land* (1926). The gentle susurration of the leaves in the trees, and their cool green shade, contrasts with this evidence of the farmer's toil. The Moat creates a barrier between us and evidence of this activity, so that we become mere voyeurs of the agricultural picturesque.

The line of the Moat is a right angle that describes the garden's northern edge from the White Garden to the corner summer house and then most of the eastern boundary, down to the Thyme Lawn and Herb Garden. A row of old oaks spreads along both stretches. The reflections of the trees flicker in the Moat; its dark surface is flecked with leaves and twigs. Disturbed by visiting

PREVIOUS PAGE: The twin vistas from the Dionysus statue. To the left: up Moat Walk to Sissinghurst Crescent and the Cottage Garden; to the right: through the Orchard, Yew Walk and Tower Lawn to the tower. LEFT: The gazebo was designed by Nigel and Ben Nicolson in memory of their father.

waterfowl, the water ripples in the lee of the oaks which have grown into the bank. Vita and Harold's architect, Albert Powys, designed a bridge of formal aspect for the northern branch of the Moat but Vita scrawled across the top of the paper 'Most Unsuitable for Sissinghurst'. That is because the Moat speaks of Sissinghurst's medieval heritage more than any other feature; a bridge would have compromised its historical identity.

No one knows when the first house was built here; the remains we see today date from the 1560s, when a brand-new house appears to have replaced the older one – though the old manor may have been retained for use as the 'great hall' – and became the focus of a 280-hectare/700-acre deer park set within a far larger estate. The handsome tower, constructed as a belvedere or lookout, reigned over three open rectangular courts. We still have the first court, behind the surviving entrance (service) range; the second or principal court covered part of the wide, squat rectangle we know today as Tower Lawn, with South Cottage a surviving fragment of the south-east corner of what had been a spectacular Renaissance ensemble; while the third court, extending eastwards, was more domestic in feel (this was where the medieval remnant of Sissinghurst may have been retained, though nothing of it remains today). Only the original walls still in existence provide any indication of the true scale of the vanished buildings. Sissinghurst's original garden, laid out as a cruciform, occupied part of today's Orchard. (This was where Vita found Sissinghurst's one surviving rose on the day she first visited – perhaps it was not so fanciful of her to suppose it had descended from plantings of the mid 16th century.) The new house was important enough for Queen Elizabeth I to visit in 1573,

RIGHT: Kingcups form a marginal planting to preface the view northwards along the Moat, overhung by old oaks.

and its ambitious owner, Richard Baker, was knighted soon afterwards. It was Sir Richard's niece who married a Sackville, hence the family connection with Vita which made Sissinghurst, to her, seem like destiny.

The Baker family fell on hard times in the aftermath of the Civil War (they had been Royalists) and, after the estate was portioned up between four daughters, no single family member could afford to occupy the property. It lay empty for a century until finally, from 1756 until 1763 (the Seven Years War), it was rented to the Crown to use as a gaol for French prisoners of war – up to three thousand of them at a time. (The probable layout of the three courts and garden delineated above has been gleaned from a detailed ink drawing of Sissinghurst made by one of the prisoners; it was acquired by the Trust only recently and now sits in the library.) Sissinghurst must have been a squalid and crowded place during this period, and by the time the men were sent home at the end of the war, it was described as two-thirds destroyed. It seems ironic that the 'castle' tag dates from this era, because it was the French prisoners who had dubbed it *le château*. Before then, it had been known as Sissinghurst House.

There is some evidence – a handwritten note pasted on the reverse of a watercolour of Sissinghurst by Francis Grose of around 1760 – that a fire in the late 18th century finally did for the castle as a potentially habitable house. The note suggests that most of Sissinghurst was razed to the ground in the conflagration. If this is true, much of what survived (the front range, the tower, the Priest's House) did so because it was not connected to the rest.

A new use for Sissinghurst was found from 1796, when the parish took it on and ran it as Sissinghurst Farm, essentially a rural workhouse. It proved quite a success, turning a profit on the estate's good agricultural land. Noting this, later owners tenanted out the land and buildings in the mid 19th century to a gentleman farmer, who built the fine farmhouse overlooking the front meadow, which is the head gardener's quarters

today. In the ensuing decades it was occupied by several other farming families, the last of whom allowed it to slide into near-dereliction during the agricultural depression of the 1920s.

By the time Vita and Harold appeared in early April 1930, the property had been on the market for two years without exciting much interest. This is not so surprising, considering its ruinous state and clear unsuitability as a normal family home.

But the Nicolsons, of course, were not a normal family in need of a normal home. The boys, Ben and Nigel, who were seventeen and fifteen in 1932 when the family moved in, were given quarters in the old brewhouse in the front range, north of the arch, for the periods when they were back from boarding school (Eton College). The family's meals were taken in the Priest's House, where Ben later moved into a separate room upstairs. Vita and Harold were to occupy separate bedrooms in South Cottage, while the library or Big Room was in theory a communal space, also intended for entertaining (though there was not much of that, so the room was barely used). The tower was where Vita had her study, on the first floor, a very private domain where Harold rarely ventured.

Constant intimacy does not suit every family, and according to Nigel Nicolson, the arrangement was agreeable to all: 'They had achieved by the accident of the physical separation of the buildings the perfect solution to our communal lives. Each of us could be alone for most of the day, and we could unite for meals.'

These dispersed living quarters meant that the family had to spend quite a lot of time outside, as they moved from one isolated space to the next – something which did not bother Vita (except in midwinter) but

RIGHT: The old brick wall – perhaps the oldest at Sissinghurst – with wallflowers in the bed at its foot and pale yellow Corydalis ochroleuca *growing from the crevices.*

slightly irked Harold. It did mean that, like it or not, life at Sissinghurst truly was an indoor-outdoor experience.

In 1946 Harold more surely integrated the south end of the Moat into the overall design by placing the garden's key statue, of the Greek god Dionysus, on the far side of the water, backed by a curving hedge of beech. Dionysus's pose is rather lithe and sexy, and possibly slightly 'camp'. Camp is now something of a taboo word, in the context of the reclamation of the term 'queer' to mean anything or anyone that is other, different, hybrid or out of the mainstream. Camp still has its uses, perhaps, if employed carefully to denote things that are over-the-top, that display shoddy craftsmanship and revel in that, or are deliberately vulgar. There is a place for camp – it is fun, liberating and egalitarian. But it does not often make for great art. Is Sissinghurst ever camp? Nearly, especially where statuary is involved. The Sissinghurst statues are

not historically important – most were bought from local antique shops or yards – and they seem somewhat declamatory or highfalutin in style. On the other hand, they have been used sparingly and with forethought, so perhaps the fair judgment is that the garden never quite sinks to campiness. Vita and Harold were too careful, too controlled, to let that happen. It was not their style.

Dionysus marks the termination of two vistas: one down the length of the Moat Walk, potentially from as far as the Cottage Garden, and one long view from the steps of the tower and across the Orchard. The beech hedge was recently reduced to waist-height to lessen the sense of a barrier with the surrounding farmland – so that we can see how 'the woods were brown wedges in the blue Weald', as Vita put it in her novel *Family History* (1932). On the Moat itself, the battle against duckweed never ends, with a planktonic mineral application now being used, as well as extra consignments of oxygenating marginal plants to grow among the flag irises.

There is a part of the estate, near here, that started out as one of the most important aspects of life at Sissinghurst for Vita but ended up unregarded and neglected. This is the Lake – strictly the lakes, as it is made up of two bodies of water – situated down the hill and one field south of the garden. The visitor can cut across the field or follow the line of poplars which Harold and Vita planted almost immediately on arrival. The potential for a lake was one of the things that attracted Harold and Vita to the place, and they set about damming a stream to create one during the first winter of their ownership.

Sissinghurst's new Lake was an immediate success – quite an achievement given the difficulties associated with water projects. It was stocked with trout and Vita briefly took up fishing. Steps to allow for swimming were added, and it became part of the daily round for the whole family. As Vita wrote in her *New Statesman* column: 'It was a creation romantic beyond my hopes. Extravagantly

I ordered a boat from the Army and Navy Stores.' But of course it was the Lake's atmospheric quality that Vita cherished most. In the same article she revealed some of the deeper thoughts the Lake had inspired in her: 'The very reflection of trees in water suggests how true and untrue life may be: the solid oak as we see it growing on the bank, the mirrored reflection – truth in untruth, the one no more convincing than the other.'

This ambivalence about the nature of truth and authenticity played into Vita's feelings about the fragmentary nature of her own personality, which seemed to her to be made up of different, sometimes conflicting identities. The garden at Sissinghurst would become an arena where her feelings could be played out.

In her early years at Sissinghurst, the Lake perhaps meant more to Vita than anything else in the estate or garden – which was, of course, largely covered with detritus at that time. One of her poems, written in 1925, before she came to Sissinghurst, is redolent of her feelings about lakes. The stream-of-consciousness style of 'On the Lake' is unusual in the context of Vita's work as a whole and shows the influence of Virginia Woolf, with whom Vita was romantically involved in the late 1920s and whose intellectual and literary impact, as we have

OPPOSITE: The statue of Dionysus, in its beech-hedge niche, was added in 1946. ABOVE: Moat Walk from Sissinghurst Crescent, with the open expanse of the Orchard to the left and Azalea Bank to the right.

seen, was of great importance with regard to the garden. The poem relies on repetition, listing and an emphasis on single words, echoing Vita's natural pattern of speech and her clipped intonation. The effect is cumulative and textural, the tone both conversational and philosophical, while the prevailing mode is descriptive and faintly erotic. Very Vita.

> *...Peer in the water*
> *Over the boat's edge; seek the sky's night-heart;*
> *Are they near, are they far, those clouds, those stars,*
> *Given, reflected, pooled? are they so close*
> *For a hand to clasp, to lift them, feel their shape,*
> *Explore their reality, take a rough possession?*
> *Oh no! too delicate, too shy for handling,*
> *They tilt at a touch, quiver to other shapes,*
> *Dance away, change, are lost, drowned, scared;*
> *Hands break the mirror, speech's crudity*
> *The surmise, the divining;*
> *Such things so deeply held, so lightly held,*
> *Subtile, imponderable, as stars in water*
> *Or thoughts in another's thoughts.*

The Lake continued to exert a hold over Vita for almost a decade, until the war intervened. Sissinghurst was at that point subject to the attentions of the British Army, for the fields of Kent were expected to be a key battleground against Hitler's invading army, who would surely take this route towards London. Soldiers dug trenches, while Vita's beloved woods, and the Lake, would soon be despoiled by marauding tanks. Vita never recovered from this invasion by supposedly friendly forces, and more or less abandoned this part of Sissinghurst from that point on. A column she wrote in the *New Statesman* in 1939,

LEFT: Spring in the Orchard. This was a place of relaxation and freedom, away from the intensity of the garden's other spaces.

before the storm, reads as a harbinger of what was to come, if she did but know it:

> *On this particular night the moon gave no reflection into*
> *the darkened waters. The only things which gleamed and*
> *glowed were the water-lilies, whitely resting on the black*
> *pool. Taking the boat out, I cut the milky stalks of the*
> *lilies in the moonlight, and as I did so, drifting, aeroplanes*
> *appeared over the lake, chased by the angular beams of*
> *searchlights, now lost, now found again; now roaring*
> *out, now silent, traceable only by their green and red*
> *lights sliding between the stars. A fox barked at them...*
> *The fox barked again, and carrying the inert lily buds*
> *I made my way across the fields. The homely weapon*
> *of the scythe shone all along the blade where I had*
> *left it hanging among the fruit.*

The Lake, and the fields leading down to it, were also, for Vita, a place of romance and seduction. In the chapter of *Family History* which is clearly set at Sissinghurst, she describes how a pair of lovers walk through the garden and finally go down to the lake and return again through the fields. 'Once, they sank down into the scented hay and stayed there for a space, silent but for the eloquent touch of love.'

The Moat Walk is a sunken *allée* with a dead-straight grassy path that follows the line of the old moat, where it travelled along Sissinghurst's southern boundary. Harold originally imagined it would be a bowling green, that classic 17th-century garden feature, though when it had been finally cleared and turfed, in 1932, it became obvious it was not going to be wide enough, so had to be a walk. The mottled brick wall on its north side, dividing the walk from the Orchard, is part of Sissinghurst's 16th-century structure, or possibly even dates from the first, medieval house on this site, and was never to be moved or taken down; it caused Harold considerable design problems because it does not run parallel with anything

else, notably the adjacent Nuttery. In exasperation, he labelled the garden 'obtuse' at this stage. But, as ever, he made it work, creating a secret spine to the garden and another way into the Cottage Garden. Having said that, because of its 'in-between' nature, the Moat Walk is one of the most easily overlooked parts of the garden, except when the azaleas on the south side explode into colour in the spring.

The azalea bank was most likely a feature Vita copied from William Robinson at Gravetye Manor, where a bank of azaleas overlooked the formal rose garden. The fragrant flowers of *Azalea molle* (now *Rhododendron molle* susbp. *japonicum*) are of a yellow that grows richer over the weeks, ending up almost orange. They form a bank of luculent spring colour that effectively obscures the awkwardly angled boundary with the Nuttery and creates a strong and unusual sensation, as you walk along, of plant shapes – shrubs, not trees – developing above head height. The golden autumn foliage of the azaleas provides a second flush of excitement.

In Vita's time, the azaleas were chiefly the highly scented Ghent hybrids in many colours – old varieties, such as the dark purple *Rhododendron* 'Grandeur Triomphante', 'Rouge Brique', 'Josephine Klinger' (salmon pink and lemon) and 'Coccineum Speciosum' (brilliant orange: 'one of the best of all'). Beneath the azaleas is a complex understorey of fragrant ground-covering plants, such as (the invasive) *Houttuynia cordata* 'Flore Pleno' and sweet woodruff (*Galium odoratum*), alongside bulbs like the delicately arching English bluebell (*Hyacinthoides non-scripta*) and *Anemone nemorosa*. Here, too, are lilies-of-the-valley; false lilies-of-the-valley (*Maianthemum bifolium*); dog's-tooth violets (*Erythronium*); fairy bells (*Disporum* species); willow gentians (*Gentiana asclepiadea*); toad lilies (*Tricyrtis* species); and the yellow-flowered *Kirengeshoma palmata*. Also squirrelled away in here is an interesting shrub, yellow root (*Xanthorhiza simplicissima*), with exquisite little burgundy flowers.

Against the base of the old wall on the northern side Vita planted that great crevice-occupying wallflower, *Erysimum* 'Bowles's Mauve', a tradition which is kept up today, while the Portuguese squill (*Scilla peruviana*) also bubbles up from the brick. Vita sprinkled stripy zinnias here for high summer (an idea that was retried without success in 2016). Hart's tongue ferns provide a sense of continuity and that requisite dash of the wild, and *Corydalis ochroleuca* bursts out from the cracks. White wisteria – both 'Alba' and 'Shiro-kapitan' – was planted against the north side of the wall so that it washes up over the top, another Vita touch and a planting which Nigel Nicolson felt was the best in all Sissinghurst. A line of five lidded, lead urns of 18th-century appearance, purchased one at a time (as funds allowed) in the 1950s and running along the top of the wall, adds a certain panache, especially when swathed with the twirling flowers and foliage of the stately wisteria.

At the western end of the Moat Walk is a steepish flight of steps which takes the visitor up to a Lutyens bench set against a curving box hedge known as Sissinghurst Crescent. This was Harold's joke about the naming of new suburban roadways, a vocabulary he came across while serving as an MP in the 1930s. It may also have been a funny little dig at Vita because he had lost the battle of the azaleas as a choice of plant for the bank, having deemed them to be 'Ascot, Sunningdale sort of plants' – in other words, pretentious-suburban. His 'Crescent' was a way of letting his peers know that he knew what was good taste and what was not – at least in his opinion.

The bench provides a vantage point for views down the length of the Moat Walk to Dionysus. It is

OPPOSITE: Moat Walk scenes: massed yellow azaleas with English bluebells (above); the berry-like hips of Rosa virginiana *(below).*
RIGHT: Tricyrtis formosana *(above); white wisteria cascading over the wall above* Corydalis ochroleuca *(below).*

LEFT: Zinnia *Benary's Giant Series growing at the base of the wall. Vita liked zinnias here and they have been tried again — though slugs have now put paid to the experiment. ABOVE:* Gladiolus murielae *growing in one of the pots flanking the steps up to Sissinghurst Crescent.*

one of relatively few formal sitting spaces inserted into the garden, for Sissinghurst as a whole is quite a busy, perambulatory garden, as gardens made by gardeners tend to be. (Vita herself barely ever sat down in it.) The paved semicircle disguises the fact that the Cottage Garden, just behind, is not aligned with the Moat Walk, though the four Irish yews at its centre conspire to create the impression that it is.

The effect of this sudden dead-straight grass walk, overborne in season on one side only by vivid yellow and orange, is somewhat surreal – in the architectural, de Chirico sense – not least because it is quite unexpected, popping up in the middle of the garden like this, with its panoply of artefacts and lopsided nature.

It is probable that Harold, particularly, was influenced by a new baroque sensibility which was coming to the fore in fashionable and intellectual circles in the 1930s, with people like Rex Whistler, John Betjeman, Cecil Beaton and Nancy Lancaster adopting a kind of wilfully old-fashioned yet rather glamorous attitude, and a style of interior design inspired by 17th- and early 18th-century motifs, often deployed in a light-heartedly twisted manner. The aim was for a transcendent, dreamlike look informed by rococo precedent, and as such was perhaps the closest England got in the early 20th century to a home-grown form of surrealism (hence the de Chirico comparison). The look was characterised by an aesthetic of mirrors and illusion, distortion, wit, 'camp', avant-garde photographic effects, parody, costumery, theatricality, hybridity, eclecticism and faux heroics, all bound up with a certain frivolity of sensibility. The attitude was certainly associated with a homo- and bisexual milieu, though not exclusively so. The style had a rather decadent, late-period feel, perhaps suitable to a garden like Sissinghurst which, with Hidcote, might be described as a late-period Arts and Crafts garden, bending and breaking the rules laid down by earlier, professional designers.

It was a milieu in which individualist or 'eccentric' women could thrive – people like Edith Sitwell of Renishaw Hall and Lady Ottoline Morrell of Garsington Manor. And potentially Vita, as well, though she distanced herself from this world, perhaps because her own mother, Lady Sackville, had made a name for herself as an avant-garde interior designer working in a rather over-the-top manner. Vita's bedroom in the family's London house, as designed by her mother, featured vivid green walls and floors, sapphire-blue furniture, an apricot ceiling and six bright orange pots on a green marble mantelpiece. Perhaps Vita had had enough of that kind of thing. She favoured what was dark and ancient and aristocratic, not what was shiny and new. To her eyes, anything that was not Jacobean was pretty much plebeian.

Her only foray into what might be termed the neo-baroque sensibility was the White Garden, which was conceived in 1939, but made after the war. It was created under the influence of Syrie Maugham, the celebrated interior designer who favoured all-white schemes, though in truth that look was more than fifteen years out of date by the time the White Garden came into being. The Spring Garden is the other Sissinghurst feature which might be bracketed most easily with this type of attitude, along with the Moat Walk itself. It was expressed, too, in the decorative artefacts scattered across the garden, such as the eight bronze, late-18th-century Bagatelle urns which were given to Vita by her mother in 1932 (two were later sold). Such highly decorative objects intensify the dreamlike qualities of Sissinghurst wherever they are placed, as they often look both slightly incongruous and pleasingly overblown – just the sort of thing one might come across in a dream. 🦋

RIGHT: A blaze of yellow on Azalea Bank, prefaced by Siberian iris mingling with Euphorbia palustris.

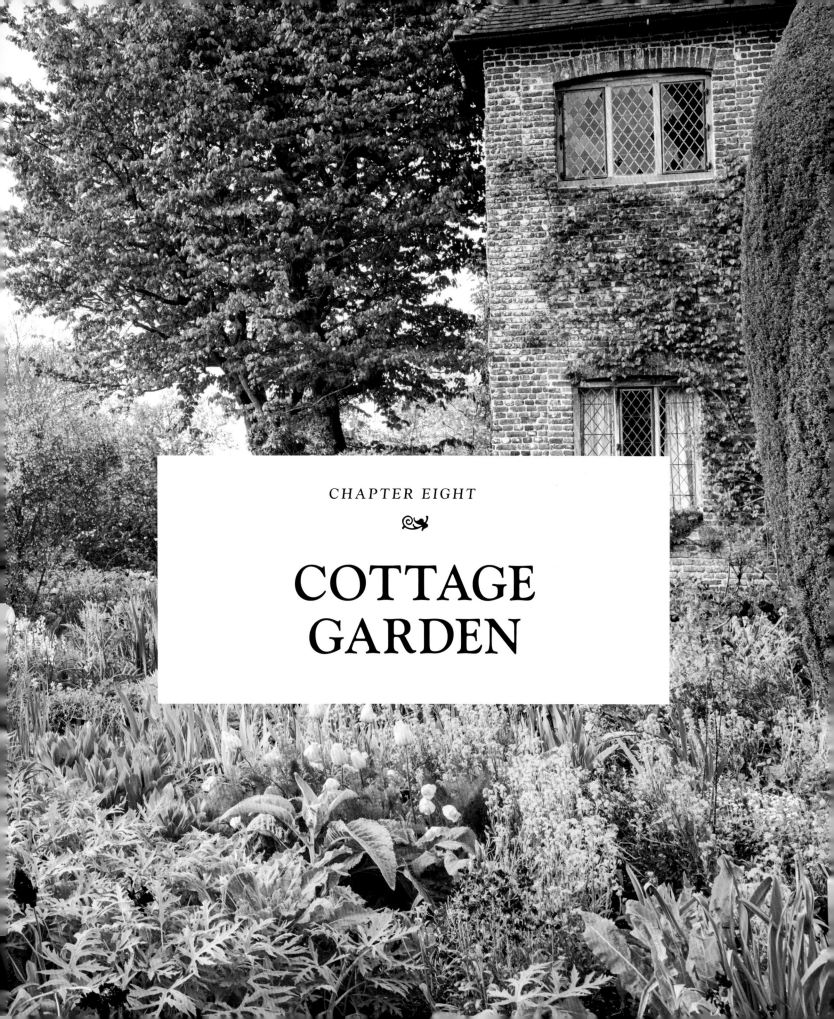

CHAPTER EIGHT

COTTAGE
GARDEN

'But in this dear delusion of a South
Which never was and never can be ours,
Drowsy, voluptuous, and rich in sloth,
We northerners must turn towards our flowers.
They are our colour; brave, they are our flags;
A living substitute for marble swags'

The Garden by Vita Sackville-West, 1946

IT IS DIFFICULT to know where to place the Cottage Garden on a guided tour of Sissinghurst. There is no 'correct' order in which to experience the garden and this hedged-in space, which might be said to be the very picture of cottaginess, can be accessed directly either from the Spring Garden and Lime Walk on its south side; from Sissinghurst Crescent at the top of the Moat Walk; or more obscurely at its north-west corner via the Tower Lawn, by the old toolshed. Soon there may be yet another way in, from the Orchard, along the eastern side of the cottage, as there are plans for a pathway here.

The Cottage Garden feels as if it sits squarely in the middle of the garden, though in actuality it does not, quite. (There are a lot of 'not quites' at Sissinghurst, which is one of its charms.) This horticulturally explosive space is in the midst of everything but somehow hidden away, for it is the most enclosed and sequestered of all the garden's episodes. There was good reason for that – this was Vita and Harold's private zone, with their (separate) bedrooms in the cottage and Harold's dark brown, book-lined study downstairs, with a casement window looking out on to the Cottage Garden. In their lifetimes the square garden in front of the cottage exuded a sense of privacy and was often bypassed by respectful visitors. As Harold observed, Sissinghurst is composed of a 'succession of privacies…All a series of escapes from the world, giving the impression of cumulative escape'. For Vita, this simple cottage was all she desired at the end of a long day writing in the tower and gardening outside. The tower gave her the frisson of romanticism and antiquarianism which added piquancy to her writing, while, conversely, the little cottage was a comforting and comfortable domestic space. Something of this is reflected in an excerpt from William Byrd's *Psalms, Songs, and Sonnets* (1611) chosen by Vita and Harold for their anthology *Another World Than This* (1945):

In chrystal towers and turrets richly set
With glitt'ring gems that shine against the sun,
In regal rooms of jasper and of jet,
Content of mind not always likes to won [dwell];
But oftentimes it pleaseth her to stay
In simple cotes enclosed with walls of clay.

PREVIOUS PAGE: The Cottage Garden in late spring, with the yellow tulip 'Mrs John T. Scheepers', wallflowers and dark purple Iris spuria *in front. LEFT: Red alstroemeria and* Dahlia coccinea, *echoed by crocosmia and the spikes of* Digitalis ferruginea *farther back; the poplars lead to the Lake.*

Today, the South Cottage, with its tiled roof and oak window frames, still exudes a pleasingly privileged and reserved air, though the atmospheric interior – including Vita's bedroom, almost unchanged – is now being opened up regularly for pre-booked guided tours for small groups.

The Cottage Garden is not somewhere to pass through or pass by, then – it is a space that seems to absorb you completely. It is the one place in Sissinghurst that feels absolutely still, the one place where there is no impulse whatever to move on to the next scene.

The two self-contained cottages standing aslant and askew amid the ruins of the old Castle proved to be ideal living quarters, since Sissinghurst was going to be above all a place for individualist fulfilment, a quiet retreat for thinking, writing and the kind of self-expression offered by gardening (where one can hide one's artistry in plain sight). It was never intended to be a gregarious or overly social environment: there were no guest bedrooms envisaged, and as time went on Vita became more and more reclusive. As Harold remarked in 1949, she would have ideally liked 'all the servants and gardeners and farm hands to be thrown into a trance like sleeping beauty, and she and her dog and the little robin by the dining room to be left as the only three moving things at Sissinghurst'. During the years of her *Observer* column (1946–61), when she wrote about almost nothing except gardening, Vita was entirely consumed by the place and rarely had visitors, though in summer there was the constant flow of the public through the garden. Their presence at times gave Sissinghurst a paradoxically crowded air, while Vita remained alone and aloof.

The possibility of a cottage garden next to this little house was immediately realised, and the simple cruciform, broken-stone and brick path system was laid down early on, in 1931. Before their arrival – in fact, even before the deeds to the house had been secured – Vita had horticulturally anointed this part of the garden by planting a rose against the south side of the cottage, to grow around the doorway. It was one of her old roses, of course, 'Madame Alfred Carrière' (1879), a noisette she described in print as 'a white rose, flushed pink, scented, very vigorous and seldom without flowers', and possessed of 'a sweet, true-rose scent'. She and Harold nicknamed it 'Mrs Alfonso's Career' in one of their little private jokes, of the kind all married couples have. This rose was also a memory of their time at Long Barn, where it had festooned the bedroom windows. In her poem 'Night' (1921), which is dedicated to Harold, Vita describes:

You branches fragile, tentative, that stretch
Your moonlit blossom to my open window,
Messengers of the gentle weald...

...Your buds against my pulses; so I lie
Wakeful as though in tree-tops, and the sap
Creeps through my blood, up from the scented earth.

ABOVE: Rosa 'Madame Alfred Carrière' was the first thing planted by Vita at Sissinghurst, against the wall of the cottage. RIGHT: Achillea 'Coronation Gold' and evening primrose, backed by euphorbia, provide a fanfare for the yew quartet and central copper pot, here planted with nasturtiums.

'Madame Alfred Carrière' is a variety which has beguiled several commentators and was very much 'of the moment' among the cognoscenti. In 1932 Jason Hill (real name: Anthony Hampton) waxed lyrical about it in his cult book *The Curious Gardener*.

In 1934 the four Irish fastigiate yews were planted in the middle of the Cottage Garden, an echo of those already seen in the Top Courtyard. Today, they are delightfully wonky and lopsided. As Sarah Raven has observed of both quartets of yews: 'If you stand in these two gardens now and imagine them without these great green pillars, they'd be half the places they are.' Positioned as a centrepiece in the middle of the four yews was a large and battered copper urn, greenish with verdigris and always planted up with a changing display of some burgeoning and overflowing flowering plant – the soft-orange *Begonia sutherlandii*, for example, or crimson nasturtiums with marigolds.

As for the rest of the planting, this may be the Cottage Garden, but the effect is hardly the rural vernacular celebrated by Gertrude Jekyll and cottage-garden painters like Helen Allingham and Myles Birket Foster. The colours most associated with a traditional English cottage garden are pinks and greys (along with green, of course). The range can be deepened by blues and purple, and spiced up with oranges, reds and yellows, but the core must consist of soft, smoky colours that sing out in the light of the evening, when the weary cottager may enjoy them after a day of toil (in theory at least). These were the sorts of pastel colours favoured in the 1940s and 1950s by Margery Fish of East Lambrook Manor – whose journalism was perhaps even more influential than Vita's at the time. She recommended these softer colours because with them, she said, you

LEFT: The beds in front of the cottage are lit up by Erysimum cheiri *'Fire King' and 'Cassini' tulips, together with the buttery Molly the witch peony* Paeonia daurica *subsp.* mlokosewitschii.

ABOVE: Cottage atmosphere: nasturtiums and tagetes in the copper pot at the centre of the yew quartet (top left); the red-hot poker, Kniphofia 'Lord Roberts' (top right); the ginger Hedychium 'Tara' (bottom left); and Achillea 'Moonshine' (bottom right).

could have 'a riot without disagreement'. Additionally, the flowers of traditional cottage plants are often smaller in size than those of hybrids bred for the nursery trade, though there are some dramatic exceptions in the true cottage-garden palette, in the form of hollyhocks and larkspurs, for example.

But if it was a cottager who made Sissinghurst's Cottage Garden, then they would have been an extremely cosmopolitan sort of rustic. Vita wanted a garden such as this to be 'a symphony of all the wild sunset colours, a sort of western sky after a stormy day'. Her plantings were therefore dominated by hot colours from geums, snapdragons, nasturtiums and pansies, with the addition of the more demonstrative shapes of achilleas, kniphofias, day lilies and helianthemums. It was all intended to be unrelentingly bright, a haven for the colours she was using sparingly elsewhere in the garden. In her article for the RHS *Journal* in 1953 Vita herself described the effect as 'an almost incongruous mixture', which captures something of its edgy ambition.

Vita rarely touched upon general principles of planting design in her newspaper column, and never produced a book describing her intentions at Sissinghurst. The closest she ever came to this was in a BBC radio talk given in 1933, just as she was setting the planting style at Sissinghurst. It was published a few years later as an essay in a collection by various hands entitled *How Does Your Garden Grow?* (1935). Under the heading 'Next Year's Border', Vita lays down four cardinal rules about the making of borders. This is the clearest recorded explanation of her own principles and it has not been reprinted since that time.

The first is: observe no rule at all. In other words, don't be afraid of muddling up the true herbaceous plants with things such as bulbs and annuals: don't be hypnotized by that very ugly and rather meaningless word herbaceous. I really prefer to call the herbaceous border the mixed border.

The second rule is: plant boldly always. In my experience one never plants a thing in sufficiently large groups, even if one does it oneself, and it is almost impossible to get a professional gardener to do it. Supposing you have six roots of a given plant, it is better to set those six roots all together in one clump than to separate them into two clumps of three roots each. The same applies to bulbs: twelve tulips together are twice as effective as six tulips in separate lots. Mass your delphiniums; mass your hollyhocks; mass your catmint; mass your pinks.

This 'mass, mass, mass' advice is an alternative mantra to 'cram, cram, cram' and is more accurate with regard to Vita's actual style. She continues:

The third rule is: consider heights...Roughly speaking, of course, one plants the tall things at the back of the border and the low things in front; but it is no bad plan to vary this system by occasionally boldly bringing forward a clump of some tall subject to diminish the monotony and perhaps also to form a kind of break between one group of colour and the next. For this kind of break the grey plants are especially valuable...

...but this leads me on to the fourth [and final] rule: consider colour...I think myself that the strong, violent reds and oranges are better eliminated from the mixed border, and kept in a place by themselves. I think also that plants with grey foliage are invaluable not only as the break between colour and colour as I was saying just now, but also as a foil to pinks and blues and purples.

Vita goes on to suggest as grey plants: santolina, artemisias of various kinds, stachys ('so much nicer under its English names of Rabbits' Ears or Saviour's Flannel'), gypsophila and lavender in both its purple and white forms. She also recommends humble rosemary in the border, for its rich green tone and varied texture. (Rosemary was not commonly grown as an ornamental plant in Vita's time.)

Vita of course followed her own advice about isolating bright red and orange flowers in the garden, by more or less confining them to the Cottage Garden, where the enclosing yew and hornbeam hedges form a kind of cage for these chromatically dangerous beasts.

Photographs of the garden in the 1950s and 1960s suggest that Vita's actual plantings did not quite live up to her zingy intentions, since they appear to be rather more traditional-cottagey than hotly Mediterranean. Nevertheless, several generations of later Sissinghurst gardeners have followed the original prescription, perhaps more faithfully than Vita herself did.

Today, the beds around the central yew quartet fizz with colour and action, dominated by yellow flowers, such as the daisy-formed *Helianthus* 'Lemon Queen', *Coreopsis verticillata* 'Grandiflora' and *Rudbeckia laciniata* 'Herbstsonne', plus contrasting yellow flower shapes from *Hemerocallis* 'Golden Chimes', the pea-like *Thermopsis mollis*, *Crocosmia masoniorum* 'Rowallane Yellow' and *Asphodeline lutea*. Of other yellow or yellowish flowers, the verbascum is a plant that seems to capture Vita's style, having something of both the wild flavour of the foxglove and the stately flair of the delphinium. They are used here: *Verbascum* 'Cotswold Queen', which Vita especially recommended, as well as *V. olympicum* and *V. thapsus*. She liked to see verbascums alongside roses, and positively admired the chromatic ambiguity of these plants: 'They are all dusty, fusty, musty in colouring – queer colours, to which it is impossible to give a definite name: they are neither pink, nor yellow, nor coral, nor apricot, but a cloudy mixture between all those.'

This kind of talk would have been disapproved of by Jekyll's school of followers. That great plantswoman had been formally tutored in colour theory and close observation of nature by Richard Redgrave, Christopher Dresser and others in the earnest and hard-working atmosphere of the Kensington School of Design (attached to what became the Victoria and Albert Museum). For her, specific plants in certain combinations could be used to produce particular aesthetic and by extension emotional effects. Vita instead championed the ideal of glorious profusion and serendipitous associations of colour and form – more in the spirit of Jekyll's friend and fellow garden-maker Eleanor Vere Boyle, a forgotten figure whose romanticism and air of effortless superiority was possibly more in tune with Vita's sensibility.

Lower down among these masses of flowers around the heart of the Cottage Garden is the jaunty *Limnanthes douglasii*, while frothing above is *Thalictrum flavum* subsp. *glaucum*. Vita grew 'Gold Plate' achilleas here (today, *Achillea* 'Moonshine' is favoured), as well as red-hot pokers (*Kniphofia*) – which Harold loathed as much as rhododendrons, though he could never talk his wife out of them. The red-hot poker varieties grown in these beds now are *Kniphofia* 'David', 'Brimstone' and 'Sunningdale Yellow'. There is rich red from the flowers of potentillas ('William Rollisson' and *P. atrosanguinea*), the dainty *Geum* 'Mrs J. Bradshaw', *Silene* (or *Lychnis*) *chalcedonica*, *Helianthemum* 'Ben Heckla' and the low floribunda roses 'Marlena' and 'Dusky Maiden'. Orange tones come from the likes of *Helenium* 'Moerheim Beauty', elegant *Lilium henryi*, from the ginger, *Hedychium densiflorum*, and *Hemerocallis* 'Burning Daylight'. All of this is underpinned by the more acid-green tones of *Euphorbia cornigera* and *E. sikkimensis*, and the textures of *Sinacalia tangutica* and soft bronze fennel.

Most of this talk is of flowers, but this is also a garden of foliage effects, not least because the plants are seen at quite close range, so the green tapestry is more evident. A *Parrotia persica* (fine autumn colour) and a *Robinia pseudoacacia* are survivors from a more substantial range of trees in this garden; most have been allowed to die or been taken out, as has happened in the Rose Garden. (A good policy overall, as there is not the room for many trees in these spaces.) There are just a few grasses thrown in, such as the finely calibrated *Pennisetum*

alopecuroides 'Woodside'. The tulip range includes orange 'Cairo', golden 'Mrs John T. Scheepers', yellow 'West Point', purplish-red 'Couleur Cardinal' (a Vita favourite) and masses of 'Black Parrot'.

The planting against the front of the cottage itself has traditionally been dominated by wallflowers – for example, *Erysimum cheiri* 'Blood Red' and 'Fire King' today – with other plants of vaguely cottagey character sporting bright colouration: *Phlomis longifolia*, vivid red *Zauschneria californica* and daisy-formed *Rudbeckia fulgida* var. *sullivantii* 'Goldsturm'. There is the sulphurous lime-coloured *Euphorbia cyparissias* and the extraordinary yellow-flowered, iris-like *Cypella herbertii*, with groups of red-hot pokers springing up, including 'Royal Standard'. The tulips here are 'Formosa', yellow with distinctive green bands, and orange-red 'Annie Schilder'. Pots of

dark aeoniums have been placed near the cottage door.

Roses appear in the wide bed on the western side of the Cottage Garden. *Rosa* 'Cantabrigiensis', with small primrose-yellow flowers, is here, with 'Frühlingsgold' in the south-west corner and the bright crimson 'Parkdirektor Riggers' looking stunning against the brickwork in the sunshine (though it does go dull in low light), underplanted with orange nasturtiums. One rose that often surprises visitors is 'Masquerade', a bright climbing variety with big flowers which resemble vanilla and raspberry ice cream swirled together. It really does not look like the sort of rose Vita may have preferred. Yet

ABOVE: Helenium *'Moerheim Beauty' lends intensity to the border, with the fluffy yellow flowers of* Thalictrum flavum *behind.*

she did. She chose it, and kept it, despite it being in fashion with the masses. Who would have guessed? It underlines the difficulty today's gardeners have when dealing with historic gardens of herbaceous material, where they must attempt to 'method act' their way into the minds of long-dead gardener-owners, much as an actor might try to inhabit the mind of a character they are playing. In this spirit, Troy Scott Smith reintroduced 'Masquerade' in 2017. Another challenging 'Vita rose' brought back into the Cottage Garden is the climber 'Gruss an Teplitz' (1897), which is a rather startling crimson.

Honeysuckles are also a feature of this western bed – vibrantly coloured types such as *Lonicera × brownii* 'Dropmore Scarlet' and *L. × tellmanniana*. This is a genus which had a stronger presence across the garden in Vita's day. Foxgloves (*Digitalis ferruginea*) and euphorbias (*Euphorbia griffithii* 'Dixter') underpin plantings that are

dominated by yellow and orange flowers in different forms: the daisies of *Coreopsis verticillata* 'Grandiflora', the perennial pea *Lathyrus aureus*, the little pansy *Viola glabella* and the distinctive bells of *Kirengeshoma palmata*. They were not a key component of Vita's repertoire but across this garden euphorbias are now prominent, with *Euphorbia cornigera*, *E. epithymoides* and the statuesque *E. stygiana* playing a dynamic role. Cannas are another innovation from the National Trust period, along with the gingers (*Hedychium*), though they are used sparingly, and only in the Cottage Garden.

Just west of the cottage is the old toolshed which has a curious little garden area attached; the roses 'Hidcote

LEFT: Iris 'Kent Pride', its strappy leaves contrasting with euphorbia.
ABOVE: In the corner, a katsura tree (its foliage turns gold in autumn), with the pleach of the Lime Walk visible over the hornbeam hedge.

Yellow' and tough *Rosa × harisonii* (both Vita plantings) can be found here above hellebores and ferns, including *Polystichum setiferum* and *Dryopteris filix-mas*. The east side of the garden harbours more semi-shady areas, where *Phlomis russeliana* and *Physalis alkekengi* grow, while a quiet woodland zone off the south-east corner of the garden, known as the Triangle, today comprises epimediums, hellebores, hostas, polygonatum, trilliums and *Uvularia* species – though this spot is easily missed.

The roses on the cottage include, on the east wall, 'Alchymist' (mixed shades of yellow, apricot, peach and gold), *Rosa banksiae* and the profuse yellow noisette 'Claire Jacquier' (1888), and on the south-west corner, to the left of 'Madame Alfred Carrière' herself, cherry-red 'Bengal Crimson'. The roses at Sissinghurst are deliberately not always deadheaded assiduously, just to emphasise the garden's apparently artless character and also, of course, for the autumn and winter hips.

The Cottage Garden turns surprisingly moody at dusk, as those strong, hot colours are dulled without the reflecting effect of the sunshine – all the yellows tinged with grey, the oranges with purple, the reds going black. Yet this garden is perhaps at its best in the middle of the afternoon in high summer, which is when Harold used to come and sit out here in his chair on the front doorstep of the cottage. Later in life he would have a nap, surrounded by colour, scent, singing birds and buzzing insects. And who would not do that? 🐝

RIGHT: Evening in the Cottage Garden in late summer, with orange Zauschneria californica 'Dublin' in the foreground, yellow linaria (left) and helenium, helianthus and hedychium also in flower.

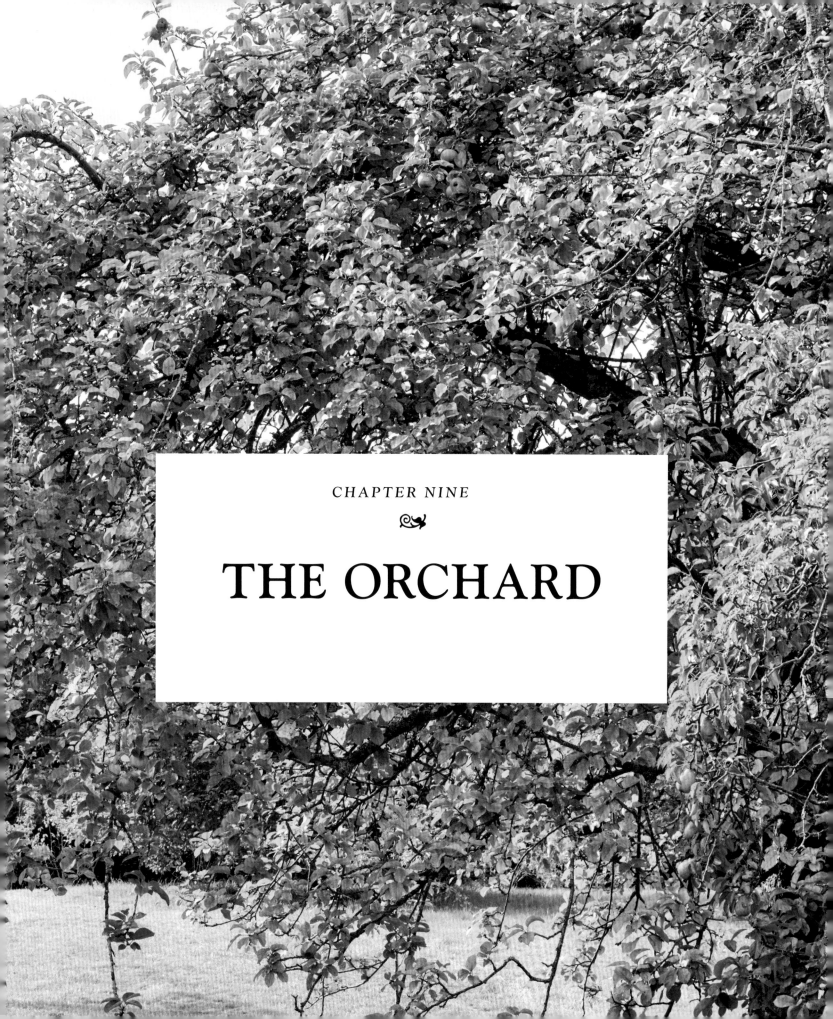

CHAPTER NINE

THE ORCHARD

*'Sometimes in apple country you may see
A ghostly orchard standing all in white,
Aisles of white trees, white branches, in the green,
On some still day when the year hangs between
Winter and spring, and heaven is full of light.'*

The Land (Spring) by Vita Sackville-West, 1926

I T WAS ARGUABLY the best design decision of all, to let the Orchard be. It takes up almost half of the space available for the garden and stands as a quiet place reserved for solitary wandering and thinking, where the horticulture, such as it is, is more relaxed and seemingly unconsidered than anywhere else at Sissinghurst. With the Orchard given its room, Sissinghurst can breathe.

Unlike productive garden areas at most grand houses, the Orchard is not an appendix, walled off around the back of things. That is because this space was never an orchard, historically, but was most likely turned over to fruit trees in the late 19th century, when even the castle's precincts were being farmed.

When Vita and Harold appeared on the scene they discovered numerous old apple, pear and other orchard trees growing here unregarded, not fruiting as well as they might and swathed in an air of benign dilapidation. They loved it and did not change it. In fact, they attempted to enhance the existing atmosphere by allowing the grass to grow long and sowing more bulbs and wild flowers,

PREVIOUS PAGE: A number of old trees were lost from the Orchard in the great storm of 1987. Today, it is a mixture of young and mature specimens. LEFT: Rosa 'Blush Rambler' climbing up an orchard tree.

and then – perhaps the gardening innovation for which Vita is best known – deliberately growing climbing and rambler roses up and over the orchard trees.

Vita was not the first to do this (Gertrude Jekyll had recommended it) but she pushed it farther than anyone else hitherto. As ever, Vita's gardening example came from William Robinson's Gravetye Manor, where she recalled how 'high up into his trees he flung great festoons of vine, honeysuckle, jasmine, and again roses; in fact anything that would climb and cling, draping the upper branches with an unexpected beauty.'

Vita's favourite rose for growing up the apple trees was 'Madame Plantier' (1835), which has bundles of gorgeously voluptuous flowers that begin a delicate pink and then turn white, with the faintest hint of cream. It grows in the Orchard to this day.

There are all kinds of horticultural problems associated with growing roses on trees. It is not particularly good for either of the plants involved, and old or weakened trees in particular are liable to be strangled quite quickly by the entwining rose stems, losing whatever health they may still be clinging on to. Vita would have said that it was worth it, given the effect of trees swagged and festooned with flowers. Today, the

THE ORCHARD 159

Orchard roses are either grown on 2.7-metre/9-foot chestnut poles, away from the trees, or else they are allowed to clamber up mature, healthy trees – but only on the north side, to minimise any damage.

The vision of roses and apple trees set in greensward was imprinted on the minds of Harold and Vita from their very first visit, when they came across a gallica rose growing in the old Orchard. It would not have been flowering when they first saw it, but when it did, the flowers came out as small, perfect circles in a clear mid purple. This was one of the forgotten 'old shrub roses' which Vita, Edward Bunyard, Constance Spry and others were engaged in resurrecting. Not knowing its true identity, Vita and Harold named it 'Sissinghurst Castle', the name by which it is still known (although some rosarians think it to be 'Rose des Maures').

Harold immediately understood that it would be best if the Orchard was treated differently to Sissinghurst's other garden episodes. This was his capital stroke – to leave it apparently untouched, as a void to balance the fullness elsewhere. As Vita commented: 'Too severe a formality is almost as repellent as the complete absence of it.' This is a garden which constantly expands and contracts in the mind's eye as the visitor walks round. When you arrive at the Orchard, the garden at Sissinghurst suddenly seems to be very large indeed; it is almost as if it acts as the 'garden' to this collection of 'garden rooms'. There was to be a tonal difference, too. Harold wrote to Vita of his vision of 'dells, boskies [*sic*], tangles' formed by little groupings of musk roses and other flowering shrubs among the orchard trees, surrounded in spring by a variety of bulbous plants. Informal, winding paths were made through the grass

LEFT: The view back towards the Cottage Garden, with Narcissus poeticus *thriving in the long meadow grass.*

ABOVE: In the meadow: a wild orchid (top left); snake's head fritillary (top right); autumn crocus (bottom left); and naturalised narcissus (bottom right).

and Vita enthusiastically planted gentians, fritillaries and hundreds of daffodils. Later, she would glory in what she described as a sea of gentians surging at her feet. This was a plant she had 'inherited' from William Robinson.

The atmosphere and attraction of the Orchard as a feature of her beloved Kentish countryside was encapsulated by Vita in one of her seasonal 'Country Notes' columns in the *New Statesman*, written in the autumn of 1938:

> *The hedgerows are already hung with the black and red*
> *clusters of shining blackberries, and the nuts in their pale*
> *green sheaths are more abundant than I have seen them*
> *for many years. The fallen maggoty ones crack underfoot*
> *as we tread, reaching up to pull down the sound ones*
> *hanging overhead. The little white umbrellas of the*
> *mushrooms are dotted all over the fields. On the garden*
> *walls the peaches are no less rosy than the bricks, and*
> *the figs have turned as brown as a piece of old velvet.*
> *Out in the orchard, standing just high enough to have*
> *escaped the May frosts that ruined the blossom in the*
> *valleys, big green cooking apples drop with a thud into*
> *the grass among the violet cups of the autumn crocus.*

The sole note of formality here would be the classical column base known as the Shanganagh, which Harold had brought back from Shanganagh Castle, his uncle Lord Dufferin's residence in County Dublin, Ireland. With an inscription related to the Reform Act of 1832, it is the only artefact at Sissinghurst that seems to come from this world, as opposed to 'another world than this'. The gardeners call this ornament 'the humbug' because of a plaque affixed to it which reads, 'Alas, to this date a humbug' – as a later refutation of the Act. 'The humbug' seems somewhat misplaced in this garden of dreams, but at least it is consumed by the Orchard. Previously, the plinth was surrounded by roses in a rather formal manner, but now the grass is allowed to grow right up to the base.

ABOVE: Rosa 'Félicité Perpétue' appears three times in the Orchard, along with around twenty other old-rose varieties, including 'Madame Plantier', 'Mrs Honey Dyson' and 'Adélaïde d'Orléans'.

If one stops to think, the idea of wandering around the long grass of an old orchard, with fragrant roses above and bright flowers below, is one of the most intensely romantic experiences imaginable, especially if one is accompanied by the object of a first flush of love (or lust). Of course, Vita revelled in the hesperidate fantasy, identifying the special atmosphere of the Orchard with her own innermost dreams and desires. Her long poem *The Land* sums up the intoxicating appeal of plants such as snake's head fritillaries, which she planted here in abundance:

> *And then I came to a field where the springing grass*
> *Was dulled by the hanging cups of fritillaries,*
> *Sullen and foreign-looking, the snaky flower,*
> *Scarfed in dull purple, like Egyptian girls*
> *Camping among the furze, staining the waste*
> *With foreign colour, sulky-dark and quaint,*
> *Dangerous too, as a girl might sidle up,*
> *An Egyptian girl, with an ancient snaring spell,*
> *Throwing a net, soft round the limbs and heart…*
>
> *…And I shrank from the English field of fritillaries*
> *Before it should be too late, before I forgot*
> *The cherry white in the woods, and the curdled clouds,*
> *And the lapwings crying free above the plough.*

Vita shifts the tone from the pastoral to the erotic and back again with ease, blurring the focus and eliding the two, just as she did in life, for the Orchard was yet another venue of seduction for her. As always she is also partly writing about herself in this description of the 'snaky flower' which is somehow one and the same with

RIGHT: The snake's head fritillary was a special plant for Vita, who extolled it for its sly beauty and exotic frisson.

the captivating Egyptian girl, 'sullen and foreign-looking'. With her aquiline nose and dark countenance, that was also the Vita look. Her first love, Violet Trefusis, recalled Vita's 'deep stagnant gaze' even as a twelve-year-old girl.

For another of Vita's lovers, Virginia Woolf, the Orchard was clearly a part of Sissinghurst which had a special, romantic intensity of meaning for her, since she wrote of it to Vita in a message of March 1941, shortly before her suicide: 'I suppose your orchard is beginning to dapple as it did the day I came there. One of the sights I shall see on my death bed.'

The Orchard today remains in a state of transition, having been gradually replanted in stages after the loss of large numbers of older trees in the great storm of 1987.

There are a few old oaks dotted about, and a handful of old apples and pears, but the majority of the trees are of fairly recent planting. Of apples there are classic varieties, such as *Malus domestica* 'Egremont Russet', 'Worcester Pearmain' and 'Blenheim Orange', along with dozens of others which are worth listing for the beauty of their names alone: 'Cornish Aromatic', 'Keswick Codlin', 'Laxton's Epicure', 'Dummellor's Seedling', 'Allington Pippin', 'Kentish Quarrenden', 'Brownlee's Russet', 'Mabbott's Pearmain'. For the horticulturist of antiquarian bent,

OPPOSITE: The berry-like fruit of the crab apple Malus hupehensis.
ABOVE: Apple blossom frames the tower.

wandering around among such trees is a kind of heaven. Sissinghurst can be a garden of simple pleasures as well as complex emotional interactions. Of pears there are *Pyrus communis* 'Doyenné du Comice', 'Uvedale's St Germain', 'Catillac' and the more prosaically named 'Beth', and there are also plums and gages to be found.

In one sense the Orchard can be bracketed with the Rose Garden at Sissinghurst, because Vita retained it partly for historical reasons. Her rosarian mentor Edward Bunyard was most famous as a connoisseur of historic fruit varieties, his books standing apart as guides to the best kinds of fruit available for growing and eating at dessert. Bunyard was doggedly persevering with the Victorian tradition of appreciating fruit for its own sake, picked fresh from tree or bush and then carefully dissected using a dessert knife and fork. Partly out of respect for him, Vita could never have had the orchard trees grubbed up to make way for some new formal garden episode. Then there was the utilitarian appeal of an orchard – for the fruit, certainly, but also for haymaking. One of Vita's *New Statesman* articles published in 1939 begins: 'A few nights ago I was out scything and raking a late crop of grass in the orchard…' Vita was keen on scything, that old country skill.

Flowering cherries, too, were planted in the Orchard. This interest arose in part from Vita's respect and affection for another elderly gentleman: her friend and Kentish neighbour, Collingwood 'Cherry' Ingram, who had reintroduced delicate old Japanese varieties such as *Prunus* 'Tai-haku'. Vita planted this and it grows still in the Orchard alongside others such as 'Ukon' and 'Pink Perfection'. But there is no longer any 'Kanzan', the ubiquitous street tree which Vita mistakenly planted originally and which Cherry himself hated with a passion.

The roses now dotted about the Orchard are generally of a rambling or hedgerow character. Of white-flowered varieties, most prominent are 'Bobbie James' (rediscovered in the eponymous gardener's Yorkshire

garden by Vita's old-rose colleague Graham Stuart Thomas), 'The Garland' (Jekyll's favourite rambler), 'Madame Plantier' (Vita's original choice), the foaming 'Wickwar' and the classic 'Félicité Perpétue' (1828), which was named after two early Christian female martyrs. (The concept of female martyrdom would have appealed to Vita; she wrote several historical biographies of tragic female saints and compromised ladies of the *ancien régime*.) *Rosa* 'Mulliganii', the same rose used on the arbour in the White Garden, is left to spread itself over quite large areas. Among the pink-flowered roses here are 'Abbotswood', 'Scabrosa', *Rosa roxburghii*, deep pink 'Morletii' and the wild rose *R. multibracteata*.

The path system in the Orchard is still mown, but it has been much simplified since Harold and Vita's time. This makes sense, given the age of the trees and the relative openness of the Orchard today. It now feels more like one large feature, as opposed to a series of subdivided spaces. Then there is always the presence of the tower overhead, anchoring everything, reeling the visitor in. The north and east sides of the Orchard give on to the Moat, which offers up its own pleasures, while in the north-west corner is an elegant boathouse, constructed in 2003 in memory of Nigel Nicolson.

Bulbs have become less of a feature here in recent years, for the perfectly understandable reason that visitors have not been there to enjoy the early spring display, as the garden has been open in the summer months only. But now that regime has changed, with weekend openings across winter and into spring, and there are plans for a return to the concept of a spring-flowering orchard. In any case, there have always been large groups of pheasant's-eye daffodils (*Narcissus poeticus*)

RIGHT: It was important to Harold and Vita that the farm-like qualities of Sissinghurst should be maintained so that the whole enterprise did not seem too frivolous; the productive Orchard helps to fulfil that promise.

thriving here in the buttercup-rich meadow; they are lifted and divided every year.

The Orchard is a place where the visitor can stop for a moment to take stock, to contemplate what has been and what is to come, or to think about matters entirely unrelated to the garden at hand. The opportunity for inwardness is part of the purpose of a garden. Being at Sissinghurst can be quite an intense experience, and a meditative stroll in the simplicity of the Orchard can feel like a release. As Vita wrote in *The Land*:

> *She walks among the loveliness she made,*
> *Between the apple-blossom and the water*

Sometimes, that can be enough.

LEFT: Narcissus in the dawn light of the Orchard meadow, with the dovecote and corner gazebo in the background.

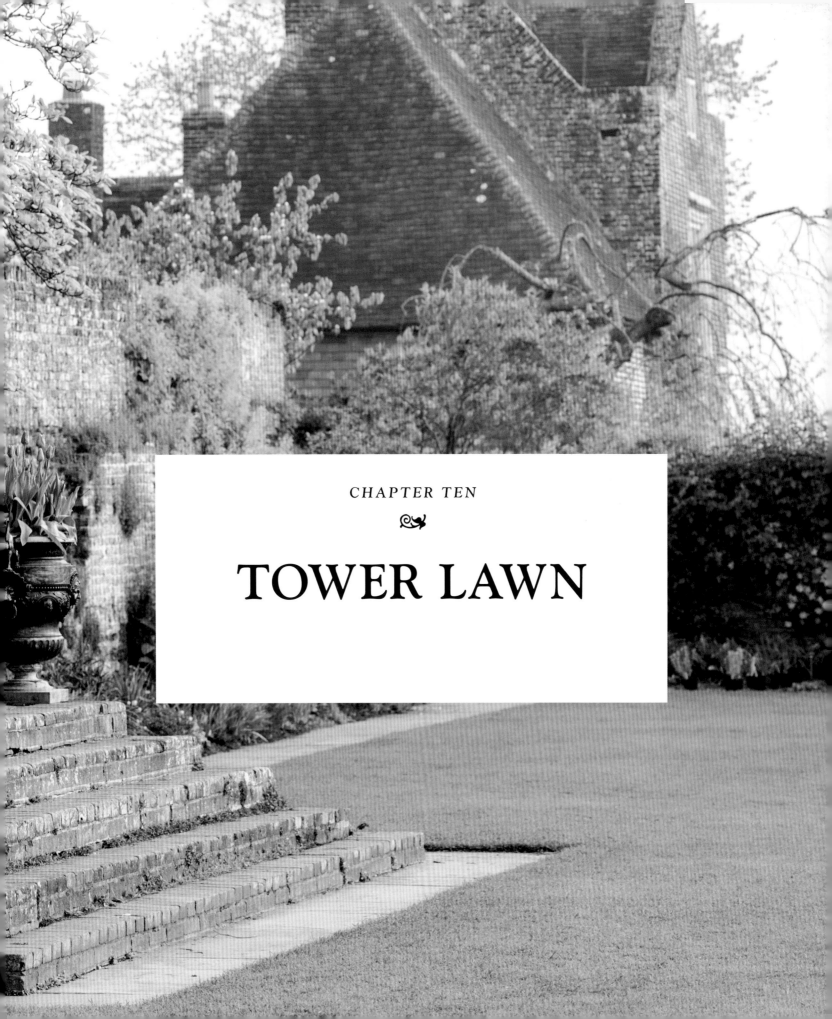

CHAPTER TEN

TOWER LAWN

'I wandered shoeless in the galleries;
I contemplated long the tapestries,
And loved the ladies for their histories
And hands with many rings.'

'To Knole' by Vita Sackville-West, 1917

A TRUNCATED and uncertain space, sunk down at the foot of the tower, the Tower Lawn – or Lower Courtyard, as it is also known – is the strangest of Sissinghurst's garden rooms. Its dislocated, 'in-between' feel arises from a discrepancy of scale which occurred after the castle was dismantled in stages during the late 18th and 19th centuries.

What is now the Tower Lawn was originally the western portion of the grand second court, with which the tower itself was then in scale. No longer. The buildings that once surrounded the court have long gone and what was its open centre is now in large part taken up by the Orchard, with Harold's Yew Walk cutting directly across it. This change in layout and proportion means that the Tower Lawn will always feel too broad and too open, an impression which is only exacerbated by the dominating presence of the tower.

Yet as with so many 'problems' at Sissinghurst, this has been turned to the garden's advantage. The unifying presence of the tower seems to make sense of all the

PREVIOUS PAGE: 'Mistress Grey' tulips in a pair of bronze Bagatelle urns, from a set of eight that were a gift from Vita's mother. Clematis montana flowers behind. LEFT: Magnolia denudata blooms by the tower.

different axial views and walks that Harold felt obliged to concoct, while the shape of the space means that it can act as a hinge, of sorts, at the centre of the garden. This helps us to negotiate the palpable atmospheric differences between the various episodes. From here, we can pivot to almost any part of the garden. The Yew Walk speaks, too, of Vita and Harold's initial impulse when they came to Sissinghurst. Aerial photographs of the early 1930s show it as an open and undefined plot. They immediately set about redefining the boundaries – surely crucial to anything that might be termed a castle.

As for the tower itself, this is the emblem of Sissinghurst. It was the tower that survived, even as the surrounding buildings fell down around it, and it is the tower which will likely survive if ever (heaven forbid) these famous gardens lie abandoned. It stands proud today, with a flag on its flagpole fluttering as a symbol of its resurrection. The presence of the tower is so strong that it may be difficult to credit the fact that its footprint on the ground is smaller than that of either the South Cottage or the Priest's House.

For Vita, the tower was Sissinghurst's HQ, the control room, her private study and haven, where entry was strictly by invitation only. As Nigel Nicolson wrote:

'This was her secret life, the life of the tower, into which we never attempted to penetrate.'

The tower could be a place of benign surveillance, as captured in this description in Vita's 1932 novel, *Family History*: 'Later they climbed the seventy-five steps of the tower and stood on the leaden flat, leaning their elbows on the parapet, and looking out in silence over the fields, the woods, the hop-gardens, and the lake down in the hollow from which a faint mist was rising.' This is not something Vita ever did with Harold. She liked to reserve the experience for her female guests, who tended to be the only people invited upstairs. Today's visitors can also enjoy the privileged view; it is one of Sissinghurst's unusual sensations, this ability to look down into the garden and to see the layout in its entirety.

A room in a tower can also be a prison, of course. That idea allowed Vita to play with the martyrdom complex she indulged in; she wrote several books on the

lives of visionary female saints and heroic but doomed figures, such as Joan of Arc. There was usually some kind of erotic undertone to Vita's literary output; Woolf referred to Vita's 'sleepwalking servantgirl novels', which she (quite generously) supposed she felt compelled to write to pay for school fees.

Yet the blissful paradox for both Harold and Vita was that, for them, the walled and barred Sissinghurst was the very opposite of a prison. It offered freedom from the cultural mores of their Edwardian backgrounds, from gender stereotypes, from the social whirl, from the constraints of professional life (for Harold), from London (for Vita), from the expectations surrounding parenthood. Crucially, it also offered up a form of (architectural) redemption in the aftermath of the death of the dream of Knole. For both of them, it was a place where they could breathe and think and read and make a garden…and perhaps be most nearly themselves.

The tower can also be understood more broadly as an emblem of Vita's status as an emancipated woman who had freed herself from some of the constricting gender expectations of the age. It stands triumphantly as a feminist refutation and reclamation of the phallic symbol which this tower – any tower – must represent. (This idea is usually associated with Freud, but Vita would have been familiar with the trope in the writings of everyone from Chaucer to Tennyson to Yeats.) It is as if the tall room in the tower, so redolent of Vita's own personality and indisputably hers alone, is a supercharged version of what Woolf had envisaged in her most famous essay, 'A Room of One's Own', published in 1929. One wonders whether this was playing on Vita's mind when she first went to Sissinghurst, six months after that

*ABOVE: Grape hyacinths (*Muscari*) fill the urns in spring.*
RIGHT: The vista from the Tower Lawn through the Top Courtyard to the entrance gate, here with scented-leaf pelargoniums in the urns.

essay appeared. For who could imagine a better 'room of one's own'? Vita was already well-acquainted with Woolf's concept even before it appeared in print, as she had accompanied her on a visit to Girton College, Cambridge, in October 1928, where Woolf read an early version of the essay as a lecture. (She had given the same lecture six days before to the young women at Newnham College, whom she had found to be arrogant, ageist and disrespectful – so perhaps she felt she needed the moral support of a female contemporary.)

The indomitable garden bubbles up at the foot of the tower. The sudden change of level on the east side of the tower arch often takes people by surprise, since it necessitates a flight of five brick steps down to the lawn. This instils a strong sense of progression through the spaces of the garden. (Sissinghurst's two arches are important to its layout: it is notable that Harold included them in his list of the garden's 'succession of privacies', along with the garden 'rooms'.) A pair of Lady Sackville's characterful bronze Bagatelle urns is placed at the top of the steps and planted up seasonally. The tower overbears the space but a feeling of balance is established by the presence of a specimen of *Catalpa bignonioides* set in the lawn in the north-east corner of the garden, its almost translucent leaves preventing it, in turn, from overbearing the space. The Tower Lawn almost feels like a vestibule, since there are ways into the Rose Garden to the south and the Orchard to the east, as well as back through the tower arch into the Top Courtyard. For most people, though, the Tower Lawn is the prelude to the White Garden, entered via the doorway on the north side, which is much the best way in (better than via the Yew Walk, or from Delos, or the North Garden).

LEFT: In the shadow of the tower: Dicentra formosa *(top left); the flower of* Catalpa bignonioides *(top right);* Magnolia liliiflora *'Nigra' (bottom left);* Rosa *'Albertine' (middle);* Eucomis pallidiflora *with salvia (middle right); and* Clematis montana *(bottom right).*

On either side of the tower arch are two long beds filled with distinguished old shrub roses and clematis, and some of the most interesting perennial plants in the garden. The arch itself is festooned with roses: 'Gloire Lyonnaise' (slightly lemony white flowers) and the very old (1830) but unburdened noisette 'Desprez à Fleur Jaune' – white with hints of yellow and pink – on the north side, with white 'James Bourgault' and a lovely free-flowering Banksian rose on the south. Roses continue at intervals in both of the beds flanking the tower. In the northern section there is the pale pink climber 'New Dawn', crimson china rose 'Cramoisi Supérieur' (1832) and then that pink classic 'Old Blush' (aka *Rosa* x *odorata* 'Pallida') in the corner; in the southern section there is 'Mrs John Laing' (pink and autumn-flowering), rambler 'Albertine' (flowers going from apricot to pink), the old gallica 'Du Maître d'Ecole', bred in Angers in 1831, with crimson-purple petals fading to ash at the edges, and in the south-west corner, another 'Gloire Lyonnaise'.

Mingling with the vines in the northern bed are *Clematis* 'Elizabeth' and the twining oriental bittersweet, *Celastrus orbiculatus*, along with shrubs, such as *Ceanothus* x *delileanus* 'Gloire de Versailles' and the white-flowered evergreen *Parahebe catarractae*. Pink and soft mauve shades are the principal colour range, with bright pink-orange *Hesperantha coccinea* 'Sunrise', purple-pink *Anisodontea capensis*, the purple annual *Legousia speculum-veneris,* the purple thistle *Galactites tomentosa, Diascia fetcaniensis* and most noticeably in high summer, *Lupinus elegans* 'Pink Fairy', a delicate lupin with a base colour of white, with purple moments. There are strong contrasts in form from *Fuchsia* 'Checkerboard' and *Hemerocallis* 'Pink Damask'. The creamy lime-green spikes of *Eucomis pallidiflora* provide a foil, along with leaves from *Bergenia* Ballawley hybrids. In spring, there are irises ('Ledger') and, later, the red-flowered bulb *Tigridia pavonia*.

South of the arch the 'Pink Fairy' lupin is continued, while the clematis used here is 'Étoile Rose'.

The spreading bush clover *Lespedeza thunbergii*, *Syringa pubescens* subsp. *microphylla*, *Melianthus major* and the dusty sage-grey *Helichrysum petiolare* help create structure. The colours here become somewhat stronger, with purple-red *Penstemon* 'Schoenholzeri', bright purple *Geranium* 'Dilys', violet-pink *Diascia rigescens* and the pink hanging flowers of *Dierama pulcherrimum*. Daisy-flowered *Argyranthemum foeniculaceum* provides a soft landing, while in spring there is the shapely *Iris* × *robusta* 'Gerald Darby'.

The northern end of the garden is divided into two beds on either side of the entrance to the White Garden, a portal known as the Bishops' Gate because of the plaque next to it, which Harold brought back from Constantinople in 1914; it depicts three bishops. On the left, in the north-west corner, there are the clematis 'Constance' and 'Étoile Rose' mingling with the roses – from the corner, moving right: climbing 'Cupid' (with lovely hips), 'Emily Gray', with loosely held yellow petals, and the vigorous 'Irish Elegance'. One unusual plant here is *Eryngium proteiflorum*, with a protea-like flower, and there is also that intriguing sage, *Salvia atrocyanea*, and the Cape fuchsia *Phygelius* × *rectus* 'African Queen'. Part of this bed was made into a 'living desert' by Vita and remnants of it persist in the gravelly soil – the South African sore eye plant (*Boophone disticha*), *Puya chilensis*, various succulents. Bulbs include *Eucomis comosa*, with striking, wavy-margined leaves, vivid scarlet *Gladiolus watsonioides* and, later, *Nerine bowdenii* 'Marjorie'. Thistly *Carlina acaulis* subsp. *caulescens* provides late-summer interest. To the right of the Bishops' Gate is a Judas tree (*Cercis siliquastrum*), while the roses are (left to right) 'Comtesse du Cayla' (unusual orange-pink petals),

LEFT: The barred window above the Lion Pond reminds us that Sissinghurst was once a gaol. Hoheria lyallii *(a Vita choice) flowers on the right, above the foliage effects of* Darmera peltata *and the fern* Osmunda regalis. Clematis tangutica *is flowering on the wall.*

Rosa lucieae, *R. spinosissima* 'William III' (bright crimson flowers with gilded stamens) and, in the corner behind the catalpa, pale yellow 'Lady Hillingdon', an old Vita favourite from her Long Barn days. The clematis is 'H.F. Young' and there are underplantings of the blue, pansy-like *Commelina tuberosa* Coelestis Group. *Lobelia tupa* is an example of a contemporary plant which the gardeners believe Vita would have grown, had she known it. *Kniphofia* 'Strawberries and Cream', meanwhile, comes out more like orange sorbet. Bulbs include purple-red *Gladiolus* 'Robinetta' and *Agapanthus* 'Findlay's Blue'.

Occupying the south-west corner of the Tower Lawn is the Lion Pond, which Vita and Harold installed at their arrival in 1930 and finally gave up on nine years later. This small, square pond was reinstated in 2018 and is now a most effective feature, with the sound of the water trickling out of the lion's-head spout. It is a gently melancholy, bittersweet spot.

Horticulturally, a suitably bog-like atmosphere is created here by the ferns *Osmunda regalis*, *Asplenium scolopendrium* Crispum Group and the connoisseurial *Phegopteris connectilis*, mingling with *Iris chrysographes* hybrids. Growing above is a *Magnolia* × *soulangeana* 'Brozzonii', with *Rosa* 'William III' against the wall. There is drama from thrusting eremurus, rich red *Lobelia cardinalis* 'Queen Victoria', *Phygelius aequalis* 'Yellow Trumpet' and palest yellow *Kniphofia* 'Little Maid' (which has been grown in this spot for decades). Less demonstrative are the oddly daffodil-like perennial *Roscoea cautleyoides*, *Anemone nemorosa* 'Vestal' and the Asian bleeding heart *Lamprocapnos spectabilis*. The view through the barred and moss-grown window above the pond, into the Rose Garden and its blossoms, is one of the most memorable in all Sissinghurst. 'How odd to come across prison bars, here,' we might think to ourselves. But we are mesmerised – the incongruity does not occur to us because Sissinghurst stands as a world apart and is a law unto itself.

The south-east corner of the garden, on the way to the Cottage Garden, is known as the Magnolia Bed, first established in 1934 and now with a group of mainly *Magnolia denudata*, along with *M. kobus* × *stellata* and *M. liliiflora* 'Nigra', the last with distinctive rich pink flowers, resembling a flock of birds-of-paradise. (There is an echoing *M. denudata* on the north side of the Tower Lawn.) Growing beneath, within a low clipped-box hedge, is the fern *Blechnum cordatum* and jagged-leaved *Rodgersia podophylla*, while a group of *Cardiocrinum giganteum* (giant Himalayan lily) planted by the doorway seems to beckon you in from the Rose Garden. In her column Vita said that while cardiocrinum is 'too splendid to be called vulgar, she is still very decidedly over life-size'. (A plant after Vita's heart.) Subtle little plants easily missed around here include the gorgeous white shooting stars of *Dodecatheon dentatum* and the diminutive blue flowers of *Omphalodes cappadocica* 'Cherry Ingram', while growing against the wall and in crevices are *Campanula poscharskyana* and the climbing snapdragon, *Lophospermum scandens*. More noticeable, perhaps, are the amazing ginger *Hedychium spicatum*, the purplish bleeding heart *Dicentra formosa* and *Hemerocallis* 'Red Breast', as well as peonies and *Anemone hupehensis*. There are roses, of course – 'Narrow Water' by the door, growing with the cardiocrinums, and 'Paul's Lemon Pillar' in the corner – with *Clematis montana* var. *rubens* 'Tetrarose' and groups of stately eremurus.

The east side of the Tower Lawn is defined by the Yew Walk, which is generally considered to have been made too narrow by Harold. It does not function particularly well as a walkway, since it is single-file only and the hedges are tall. But the vistas along it are highly effective and add to the garden's surreal qualities. The height has recently been reduced to 1.9 metres/6 feet 3 inches and the levels evened out. The Yew Walk extends almost, but not quite, from the northern end of the garden to the south, following an almost, but not quite,

straight line. This 'almost-but-not-quite' is important at Sissinghurst. Harold laid out the garden by hand and eye, making only the roughest sketch plans. Nigel Nicolson told a story about how he was asked to hold the string for his father as he worked out the line of the walk, but that he got bored and dropped it, with obvious results. Yet the Yew Walk is better not straight – like everything else at Sissinghurst. There is a seat set into the hedge that acts as a discreet vantage point over the Tower Lawn, where the crab apple *Malus* 'Blenheim Orange' helps establish a sense of place.

This open court, with its various formal portals and atmosphere of detachment, is the epicentre of the garden's disparate parts. In its uncertainty, its in-betweenness, in its almost vacuum-like quality of absence even while it sits at the heart of things, the Tower Lawn seems to echo that celebrated line (already quoted) in Yeats's poem 'The Second Coming' (1919) – 'Things fall

apart; the centre cannot hold'. The poem resonated then, and still does, because it seems to encompass some of the cultural anxieties of Vita and Harold's time. Perhaps the Tower Lawn is expressive of the disruptive rejection of societal norms which they and others were pursuing in the first half of the 20th century. It is the uncertain heart of the garden, the centre which cannot hold, apparently always on the point of collapse or implosion.

Sissinghurst is usually described as a romantic garden, or a cottage garden writ large, and that is true enough on one level. But it is also a garden that operates on several different registers. The 'romantic' description does not quite do justice to the unique atmosphere created by a set of spaces that do not obey

ABOVE: Clematis *'Perle d'Azur'* in bloom on the west wall (north section). *The distinctive leaves of* Amicia zygomeris *can be seen on the far right.*

the rules of Arts and Crafts architectural design, where a fragmented layout and sometimes violently contrasting moods are the modus operandi. As Vita recalled of the garden when they arrived: 'The tower was not opposite the archway; the courtyard was not rectangular but wedge-shaped; the walls did not run conformably to one another but shot off at obtuse angles; projected vistas refused to adapt themselves to the desired alignment.' Harold and Vita may have attempted to 'patch it up', structurally, but Sissinghurst as a whole never ran 'conformably' – and neither did its owners.

It is usual for a house, any house, to take centre-stage in its plot, or at least for the garden to be made around it. At Sissinghurst the main house had fallen down or been removed, leaving a sequence of unconnected buildings and portions of walls. The structure which you first see at Sissinghurst turns out not to be a single dwelling place at all, but a partially inhabitable range. It acts as a thin facade, like a film set on a Hollywood lot, behind which lies what began as that 'ramshackle farm-tumble' and was later remade as a garden which bears no resemblance to historical precedent – for what Vita and Harold made is in no sense a restoration or a recreation of old Sissinghurst. The two cottages stand separately and rather curiously aslant and askew amid this illogically formed domain.

Vita was possessed by the memory of her childhood home, her birthright, so perhaps it was inevitable there would be something Knole-like about Sissinghurst, with the ghosts of its formal courts extending away from the centre, and a series of semi-formal garden compartments. There are gateways, doorways and vistas, and urns and pieces of sculpture, of the kind one might expect to see at a great house. And, of course, a tower that is reminiscent of Cardinal Bourchier's tower overlooking the Green Court at Knole. But Sissinghurst is not a copy of Knole. It is a dreamlike reversioning of it: fragmentary, allusive, somehow 'like' and, at the same time, 'not-like'.

For Vita, past and present became one at Sissinghurst and time congealed, just as it did at Knole. This atmosphere of suspended animation was intensely liberating for her and Harold, as the world outside effectively evaporated.

This all adds up to Sissinghurst. It is not an equation that balances out, and it is not intended to. It is why Sissinghurst is a great garden, while that at their earlier Kentish house, Long Barn, which is more conventional in layout, is not. It is why we should be grateful Vita did not marry Lord Lascelles, as was her option in her youth, and go and make a garden at Harewood House, in Yorkshire, which would have been grand and historical but not necessarily a work of art. Sissinghurst's exploded structure, and the voids within it which cried out to be filled, means that it seems to contain multiple mysteries at its heart. This is what makes it a greater garden, ultimately, even than Hidcote. We can never entirely know it. It bamboozles us with the illogicality of its effects and disorientations.

Vita's impulse to remake the garden of her childhood is by no means unique. In fact, it is an urge that is common to many, if not most, professional designers, some of whose long careers can be understood as a sustained effort to recapture a magical garden moment of childhood. With Vita that vision was simply much bigger, more rounded, more ambitious, more real. She wanted to remake her memory of Knole in the form of a beautiful garden. That is why she described Sissinghurst, in her poem of that name, as 'commensurate with a frustrated dream'. 🍃

RIGHT: *The vista through the Rondel in the Rose Garden to the Bacchante statue at the end of the Lime Walk.*

CHAPTER ELEVEN

WHITE GARDEN

'I do agree about the Erechtheum garden. I am not at all sure myself that we oughtn't to make it all grey and white.'

Letter from Vita Sackville-West to Harold Nicolson, 5 July 1949

THE WHITE GARDEN shimmers. It scintillates, it seduces. It is the essence of the dream that is Sissinghurst. It leaves visitors entranced, feeling as if they are in that delicious halfway state between dreaming and waking.

It is difficult to divine exactly how the White Garden operates, why it is so powerful, because its final effect is so much more than the sum of its parts. Yes, it is possible to describe the plantings, and the way the internal design of the space works; but the White Garden draws us in, in ways that barely seem knowable, since it combines deep intensity of emotion with a feeling of unaccountable lightness – almost a disembodied sensation. A visit to the White Garden on a summer's evening is one of the most transcendent garden experiences in the world, and is perhaps the main reason why people want to keep coming back to Sissinghurst, why they travel thousands of miles to see it. Why Vita's White Garden is the most copied garden in existence.

PREVIOUS PAGE: White Garden surge: the spires of epilobium, with Geranium pratense 'Plenum Album' in front and Gillenia trifoliata behind. LEFT: Allium stipitatum 'Mount Everest' mingles with hesperis in the box parterre, contrasting with the dark foliage of the young quince trees.

Vita herself did not initially conceive of this space next to the Priest's House as a 'white' garden, exactly. It should be viewed in the context of Gertrude Jekyll's comments about grey- and silver-leaved plants in her *Colour Schemes for the Flower Garden* (1908), a copy of which Vita owned and annotated. In Vita's mind, grey was to be the primary colour tone. Just after they had begun it in 1949, as the last of Sissinghurst's great episodes, she described it as a 'grey, green and white garden', which is more precise and reflects her gardener's understanding of the plant vocabulary. Later, she added silver to the list. What she and Harold had agreed they wanted were the grey-greens of artemisia, the glaucous greens of stachys and the whitish-silver foliage of cineraria and santolina, which would combine together to create the ethereal suspension in which those pale flowers can hang, seemingly, in mid air, because whiteness occupies space in a unique manner. White-flowered plantings have a different effect entirely to others – a weightlessness, a feeling that the flowers are unconnected and really not quite of this world. Experienced *en masse* in this way, white produces a hypnotic effect.

And more than any other part of Sissinghurst, the White Garden changes its character as the day progresses.

It was made for the night, perhaps even more than for the day, because it is then, from deepening dusk, that the whites come into their own, almost fluorescent in the moonlight, throbbing with life and fecundity. For we must acknowledge that the point – the *only* point – of these flowers in nature is to procreate. The White Garden is a seductive place on several levels.

All white gardens are night gardens. And Vita liked the night. Her poem *Solitude* (1938) contains some of the best poetry she ever produced; one of its stanzas runs:

Daylight despoiled me of detachment; day
Confused me through the senses and the heart;
Only with nightfall could I stand apart
And view the shaping pattern of my way.

For Vita, night-time brought a strange and severe clarity, which a garden of white plantings could only deepen and dramatise. Sissinghurst is a melodramatic garden made by and for a melodramatic personality.

White? No flower in the White Garden is white, exactly. Each harbours within the folds of its petals the ghosts of other colours – purples, greens, oranges, pinks, ochres…

As Vita knew, a 'white' garden depends on green (and grey, and silver) just as much as on white. A supporting cast of foliage effects is required for the stars of the show, the white flowers, to shine and be successful in their own right. (Try putting white flowers in a vase with nothing to offset them.) Those foliage effects range from bright greens to deep greens, dull greens to dusty green-purple sages, glaucous tones to scintillating silvers. The white flowers have their different forms and individual variations of colour, but it is the plants set around them

LEFT: Delphinium *'Galahad' in one of the large beds south of the central arbour. RIGHT: The Vestal Virgin statue shrouded by the foliage of a weeping pear, in its green and white setting of ferns, leucojum and tiarella.*

which allow the whites to express themselves — the spiky, sculptural, purplish-silver cones of eryngiums, the massive, bristly, silvery green-grey leaves of the cardoons or the dramatically branched onopordums. There were other colours, too, in the White Garden — yellows, creams, pinks, and even a rich red rose climbing over the north gate. (The garden became much 'whiter' during the early period of the Trust's tenure.) The yellow theme was Vita's choice; Harold wrote to her: 'It will require some colour. I incline to pink as in the China roses. You prefer yellow. I am quite prepared to agree to yellow since I feel it is more original, and you have a better colour taste than I have.'

As we have seen, the space now occupied by the White Garden began life in 1931 as Sissinghurst's original rose garden, with a little bit of herb garden attached. It was retained in the same form during and after the war, with blowsy effusions of big shrub roses and stately groups of delphiniums. (It is easy to forget how important delphiniums were at Sissinghurst, especially earlier on. Vita became president of the Delphinium Society in the 1950s — but by the end of the decade all the delphiniums had gone, apparently the victims of an onslaught of slugs.)

Vita thought about making a white garden — on the site of the drained Lion Pond on Tower Lawn — as early as 1939. But, after some toing and froing with Harold, she accepted that such a scheme was not horticulturally appropriate to this shady spot and it was not carried through. It was Harold who returned to the theme a decade later. In 1933 he had conceived of the Erechtheum (named after one of the temples of the Acropolis, and formed after its celebrated caryatid porch) as an addition on the eastern side of the Priest's House. It was an outdoor dining space under a wooden framework covered in vines. The 'grey, green and white' garden was

RIGHT: Harold made the northern end of the White Garden into a box parterre; the southern section is less structured, with four large beds.

originally intended as a Mediterranean-style planting to complement this classical reference, and to begin with it was even known as the Erechtheum Garden. Initially, it was intended that the grey-and-white theme would apply to the southern part of the garden alone. It was only a little later that it was transmuted into what we see today: the White Garden, a dreamily effusive expression of a peculiarly English horticultural sensibility. In her *Observer* column in January 1950 Vita describes the borders as one continuous mass of planting: 'a low sea of grey clumps of foliage, pierced here and there with tall white flowers'. It is this vision which has always informed the planting and maintenance of the White Garden. With repeats of frothing flowers, translucent plants with tall stems, clusters of spires, mounded shapes and always the grey and green foliage blurring below, the overall effect is of softness, and of shapes and colours morphing together.

The structure of the garden as a whole is a little curious, as is so often the case at Sissinghurst. The arrangement of sixteen low box compartments at the north end relates to the Yew Walk, which encloses the White Garden on its east side. The Box Garden, as it was known when Harold planted it in 1950, was perhaps the sole survival of his early (and unrealised) idea for a Yew Garden complex just east of the Yew Walk, in what is now the Orchard. As a feature, the box-hedged section of the White Garden is the nearest Sissinghurst gets to straight historical pastiche, as it is clearly based on the idea of a knot garden, in quartered form. (Indeed, Harold's original design was in four quarters; it was the National Trust which later made it into sixteen sections.)

RIGHT: Hesperis, allium and erigeron conspire to blur the sharp geometry of the White Garden's box-hedged compartments.

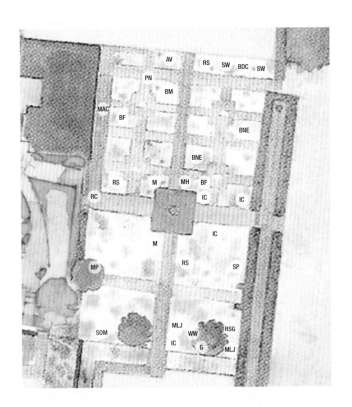

ROSES IN THE WHITE GARDEN

AV 'Aimée Vibert'
BDC 'Blanche Double de Coubert'
BF 'Blanchefleur'
BM 'Blanche Moreau'
BNE 'Boule de Neige'
G 'The Garland'
IC 'Iceberg'
M 'Mulliganii'
MAC 'Mme. Alfred Carrière'
MH 'Mme. Hardy'
MLJ 'Mme. Legras de Saint Germain'
MP 'Mme. Plantier'

PN 'Princesse de Nassau'
RC 'Cooperi'
RS *R. spinosissima* (double white-flowered)
RSG *R. spinosissima* 'Grandiflora'
SOM 'Sombreuil'
SP *R.* x *alba* 'Alba Semiplena'
SW 'Sander's White Rambler'
WW 'White Wings'

But it has a somewhat unfinished or truncated feel in this larger space. The point of this, in terms of design, can be understood only in the context of the tower. The 'knot garden' is cleverly placed at some distance from the tower while remaining visually connected with it, so that it feels like an enclosed and secret bower, with a somewhat medieval savour. It hovers at the edge of the garden like a quotation of a historical feature, somehow half-remembered. As for the enclosing evergreens, Graham Stuart Thomas once perceptively remarked that the White Garden 'would be nothing, especially in daylight, without its dark box hedges'.

The southern section of the White Garden is much simpler in form – essentially four large beds on either side of the central north–south path, allowing for a feeling of immersive envelopment among burgeoning plantings. As Vita wrote in 1950: 'My grey, green, and white garden …is, in fact, nothing more than a fairly large bed, which has now been divided into halves by a short path of grey flagstones terminating in a rough wooden seat.' The central path was originally lined with eight almond trees on the northern side, with a pair to the south, which clustered around the Ming jar that Harold had brought back from Egypt in 1937, used as a centrepiece. The almonds never performed well (possibly, in part, because Vita grew roses up them) and finally they were removed in 1967, to be replaced as a central feature two years later by a metal arbour of Nigel Nicolson's design, cloaked in the fragrant, white-flowered *Rosa* 'Mulliganii'. This arbour is celebrated as a key feature of Sissinghurst today, but to some eyes it seems a little lumpen and rather too large, squatting in the midst of the garden in this way.

LEFT: One constant in the White Garden is the Chinese vase selected by Harold as the centrepiece. Rosa *'Mulliganii' blossoms on the arbour, while* Carpenteria californica *frames the Bishops' Gate.*

Quinces (hardier) are now being grown in the White Garden in place of the almonds.

An east-west axis in this southern part of the garden, with the Vestal Virgin sculpture at one end and a small seat at the other, only adds to the visitor's feeling of being caught up in a mystery. The ground plan is unbalanced and difficult to interpret – deliberately so, for the internal organisation of the White Garden is actively designed to foster feelings of disorientation. The statue is a lead cast made in 1934 of a wooden sculpture by Toma Rosandić which is now in the library in the front range. It was tried in various sites around the garden, but in this, its final position, it has always been complemented by a weeping pear (*Pyrus salicifolia* 'Pendula') and flanked by roses, currently 'Madame Plantier'. (The original pear was blown over the hedge in the great storm of 1987 and replaced.) The statue plays into the medieval theme set by the tower, since enclosed gardens of hedges and bowers were sometimes known as Mary gardens in the medieval period, a reference to the Virgin Mary, of course, and also a signal that these were traditionally spaces associated with women. They were places of quiet repose, intimate conversations with female companions, a retreat for reading and for pastimes such as needlework and music, and occasionally for romantic assignations. All of which would have held great appeal for Vita.

Yet despite the historical associations, the White Garden does not have an antiquarian air. In fact, it seems modern. Vita was aware that white is the colour of architectural modernism, and she was also aware that pure white was a fashion in both interior design (in the work of Syrie Maugham and Eileen Gray, pre-war) and in flower design (in the books of her friend Constance Spry). White, that most impractical colour in every respect, was also a seductive post-war theme, after years of blackout and a drab grey-and-brown utility aspect to clothes and furnishings. There had been white gardens made already at Tintinhull, at Broadlands (by Lady

Mount Temple), at Crathes Castle in Scotland and at Rodmarton, while Vita and Harold's near neighbour Ian Davison had also made one in the early 1930s. (Hidcote's white garden post-dated that at Sissinghurst.) Vita and Harold had even experimented with a small yellow-and-white garden at Long Barn. But no one had attempted one at anything like this scale, or with this sort of ambition. So it was innovative, too. The statue itself was unmistakably modern, though semi-figurative, and in that sense is reminiscent of the statue chosen by Mies van der Rohe to adorn his Barcelona Pavilion (1929), a key development in architectural and garden modernism – and another hint that Vita and Harold were perhaps not as retrogressive artistically as has been assumed.

The visitor who enters the White Garden via the Tower Lawn and the Bishops' Gate is immediately plunged into Vita's 'other world'. Each part of the garden seems to act as its own little compartment: Sissinghurst is a garden that operates like a Russian doll, with scenes within scenes, and then yet more scenes within those. The large beds on each side of the path froth and bubble with certain plants that can be seen across the White Garden: *Orlaya grandiflora* (white laceflower); the little cow-parsley type *Ammi majus*; *Cleome spinosa* 'White Queen'; *Lychnis coronaria* 'Alba'; foxgloves, epilobium, hesperis, sweet peas, white rocket and honesty. Pure white annual flowers, such as *Agrostemma githago* 'Ocean Pearl' and *Cosmos bipinnatus* 'Purity', help to fill any gaps later in the season, when white verbascums (notably *Verbascum lychnitis* and *V.* 'Spica') start to play the role of the foxgloves, especially in the centre of the garden around the arbour. Perhaps the key plant is the regal lily, which Vita particularly valued, as she explained in her *Observer* column:

LEFT: The White Garden is deliberately maintained so that it appears to teeter on the edge of wild abandonment.

The tall white lilies have been a tremendous standby in the June and July garden. Their cool splendour at twilight came like a draught of water after the hot day. I like to see them piercing up between low grey foliaged plants such as artemisia, southernwood [Artemisia abrotanum], and santolina, and rising above some clouds of gypsophila, for there is something satisfying in the contrasting shapes of the domed bushes and the belfry-like tower of the lily; an architectural harmony.

Vita thought of the White Garden as essentially a June display, but today the gardeners aim to extend its season of interest from March until mid July – before they, too, let some other part of the garden take over. Vita was never particularly keen on what is known as 'succession planting' (of the kind Great Dixter, for example, is in the process of perfecting). She was much more 'all or nothing'. Nowadays, there is a big early show in spring from tulips, in varieties such as 'White Triumphator', 'Purissima' and 'Maureen'.

The bed to the left (west) of the entrance contains a range of white alliums, foxgloves, peonies and lilies, campanulas, eryngiums and white geraniums, with white vinca and spiraea as ground cover, offset by a backdrop of *Matteuccia struthiopteris* ferns. Key varieties include *Penstemon hartwegii* 'Albus' and *Phlox paniculata* 'Mia Ruys'. The wildflower feel is maintained with *Jeffersonia diphylla*, the elder *Sambucus adnata* and tiny-flowered *Vancouveria hexandra*. *Rosa* 'Sombreuil', with profuse, creamy white flowers whose petals drop freely, is on the south wall.

Near the Vestal Virgin statue the plantings become taller and more dramatic, with surging spire plants, such as foxgloves, eremurus, *Veronicastrum virginicum* 'Album' and *Physostegia virginiana* 'Alba'. Variations in form are created by *Tiarella cordifolia*, *Filipendula purpurea* f. *albiflora* and *Lysimachia clethroides*, with slender, arching flower spikes. The white pompoms of *Tanacetum parthenium* 'Rowallane' are a quintessential sight of Sissinghurst, like

miniature versions of *Hydrangea arborescens* 'Annabelle', which also appears here. There is the daisy-flowered bush *Boltonia asteroides* var. *latisquama* 'Snowbank' and the pure white bleeding heart *Dicentra formosa* 'Langtrees', all wrapped up in the contrasting textures of gypsophila and *Eryngium giganteum*. Lower down, artemisia (*Artemisia pontica* and *A. ludoviciana*) mingles with the wildling *Omphalodes verna* 'Alba'.

On the right as you enter the White Garden is a *Magnolia* × *soulangeana* 'Rustica Rubra' climbed by the rose 'The Garland'. There are more roses clustering here – a couple of rich ivory-coloured 'Madame Legras de Saint Germain', with 'White Wings' behind, and 'Iceberg' growing on the south wall (this last not grown in Vita's time, but a National Trust addition). In this bed are quantities of the white rosebay willowherb *Chamaenerion angustifolium* 'Album', while subtle colour variation is supplied by the lemony yellow Russian hollyhock *Alcea rugosa*. There are contrasting forms from the elegantly drooping stems of *Sanguisorba tenuifolia* var. *alba*, the thistly pompom balls of *Echinops sphaerocephalus*, luxuriant *Hydrangea macrophylla* 'Veitchii' and the free-standing *Clematis recta*. More floriferousness is provided by white campanulas and centaureas. There are peonies (*Paeonia lactiflora* 'Cheddar Gold': white flowers with lemon centres), the star flowers of *Anthericum liliago* and a daringly dark note from the purple markings of *Papaver* (Oriental Group) 'Black and White'. Formerly, the White Garden contained more patches of blue and soft yellow, although this has been toned down somewhat to allow the garden to sing its whiteness. There are creamy yellow shades from verbascums and eschscholzias, and

RIGHT: White – 'not so much a colour as the visible absence of colour', as Herman Melville put it in Moby Dick, *one of Vita's favourite novels.* Rosa *'Iceberg' (top left); double white* Rosa spinosissima *(middle left); alliums with tulip 'White Triumphator' (bottom left); and* Orlaya grandiflora *(bottom right). Quinces (above right) have replaced the original avenue of almond trees.*

ivory-white wallflowers, but recent experiments with blue tones (which Harold liked here) have not garnered satisfactory results in the eyes of the garden team.

Towards the arbour on this southern side the planting again surges in height, with dramatic groups of *Onopordum acanthium*, *Lilium regale* 'Album' and *Delphinium* 'Galahad'. There are white salvias (*Salvia argentea*), phlox, malvas, campanulas, centaureas, *Echinacea purpurea* 'White Swan' and the showy *Cistus × cyprius*. Daisy flowers include *Cichorium intybus* f. *album*, *Leucanthemella serotina* and *Leucanthemum × superbum* 'Beauté Nivelloise'. Slight variation in colouration is offered here again by an oriental poppy (this time 'Perry's White', with rich purple centres) and from the lemony *Scabiosa columbaria* subsp. *ochroleuca*. The roses in this part of the garden

LEFT: The tulips 'Maureen' and 'Purissima' amid wallflowers and white borage, with a camellia flowering on the wall behind. ABOVE: The metal arbour, designed by Nigel Nicolson, is adorned with 'Mulliganii' roses.

have the appeal of innocence: double white-flowered *Rosa spinosissima* by the path, 'Iceberg' up towards the arbour and 'Alba Semiplena' in the middle of the bed.

Beyond the central arbour with the 'Mulliganii' rose, the visitor enters the lattice of low box hedges, with a changing cast of dramatic players springing up from their green launchpads: *Anemone nemorosa*, *Ornithogalum pyramidale* (star of Bethlehem), honesty, white alliums and peonies, regal lilies, nigella, *Erigeron annuus*, orlaya and *Galtonia candicans* (summer hyacinth). These are now planted up as a continuum across the space, as opposed to as single species in individual beds. Roses feature strongly, of course. In the north-west corner are more of the double white-flowered *Rosa spinosissima*, 'Blanchefleur', 'Princesse de Nassau' and 'Blanche Moreau'; while in the north-east section 'Boule de Neige' dominates, with (close to the arbour), 'Madame Hardy', 'Blanchefleur' again, and 'Iceberg'. 'Madame Alfred Carrière' is planted all along the front of the Priest's

House, while at the corner, by the path to Delos, is the delightful 'Cooperi'. In Vita's day the Erechtheum was planted only with a vine (white wisteria was introduced later by the Trust); today, there is *Clematis montana* for earlier in the season and *Cobaea scandens* for later.

Against the garden's northern boundary is a bed with more foxgloves, phlox, *Filipendula purpurea* f. *albiflora* and diminutive *Deutzia crenata* var. *nakaiana*. The old noisette rose 'Aimée Vibert' (1828) grows to the left of the north door of the White Garden, flowering into the autumn, while 'Sander's White Rambler' is in the far north-west corner, with 'Blanche Double de Coubert' in front. Hundreds of specimens of the white form of *Campanula poscharskyana* grow in the crevices of the wall.

There is an exit on all four sides of the White Garden. On the west is a way into Delos, while to the north is a difficult moment in the garden's design: a rather grand gateway, with a flight of steps down, which seems to lead nowhere except towards an almost comically curtailed vista. For a period during Vita's time, the north-western part of this garden was devoted to phlox (as per Hidcote's Phlox Garden). Pines and buddleja were planted in there, and latterly a handkerchief tree (removed in the 1980s). Early on, Harold had nicknamed the space 'the cemetery', presumably because of its 'around-the-back' quality. As it stands, the shaped cupressus hedge and urn – in what is now known as the North Garden – have the effect of apparently blocking a view. To judge from photographs taken in Vita's time, the original idea was for the hedge at the garden's northern boundary to be low enough to allow for views out to the Wealden farmland. Perhaps a return to that is the solution. Either way, it all works much better if you turn around for a worm's-eye view of the White Garden, with the tower looming overhead, impossibly high. 🐝

RIGHT: The garden also includes greys and greens from the leaves and stems of stachys, artemisia, lychnis, gillenia, erigeron, achillea and a host of others.

CHAPTER TWELVE

❧

DELOS

*'So in our English garden comes the Greek
Blue wind-flow'r, cousin of the meek
Bashful anemone of English woods,
As thick as shingle strewn on Chesil Beach'*

🌿 *The Garden* by Vita Sackville-West, 1946

TO SAY THAT this part of the garden was for a long period unsatisfactory would be something of an understatement. Delos was a disaster. Every garden must have its disasters and Delos was Sissinghurst's. In her article about the garden in the RHS *Journal* in 1953, Vita described it as 'a queer amorphous area', adding 'perhaps some day it will come right.'

It all started so promisingly. Vita and Harold went on holiday to the Aegean islands in 1935 and returned enthralled by the landscape they had encountered, particularly the island of Delos, where they had seen the ruins of old houses and it had seemed to them that the stones and rubble made a kind of garden setting. That was the image they wanted to recreate back home in Kent and they set about it immediately. Their ambition, at least, was admirable, as Wealden clay is rather a different proposition to the light, dry soil of the Greek islands. A decision was made to use the stones of old Sissinghurst, which they had found lying all over the place when they arrived, as the basis for this confection, and a quantity of stone was duly barrowed into the space so that a version of the flattish rock-garden terraces they had seen could be made. They planted thymes, aubretias and saxifrages, bulbs such as iris and muscari, plus some fruit trees. But

the plants did not thrive in this north-facing site with poor drainage. As a result, Delos never convinced as a Mediterranean garden. Gradually it lost its definition as the original path, around five separate areas of rocks, was simplified and more shrubs were added, as well as a suburban-style lawn which seemed very strange in context. Finally, in 1969, most of the old stones were removed and used as foundations for the summer-house gazebo, built in memory of Harold at the corner of the Moat. Delos continued to be well maintained for what it was, but in truth it became something of a 'nothingy' area which no one knew what to do with, shrouded by tall trees like an embarrassing secret.

The failure of Delos must have been sad for Harold because it was particularly redolent for him. If it had survived, then both the Spring Garden and Delos would have been more his than Vita's. Harold and Vita both loved Greece, but for Harold, who had enjoyed a classical

PREVIOUS PAGE: Delos was restored in 2019–20 using stone from a nearby quarry and architectural fragments, including columns from a vanished Harold Peto-designed garden in Oxfordshire. LEFT: Vita and Harold's intention was that the rocks should resemble the 'platforms' made by the foundations of ruined houses on the Greek island of Delos.

education, it had a special significance. Since boyhood he had understood that Ancient Greece represented the origin of civilised society. It was his intellectual wellspring. Such a preference was not uncommon among men of his class, while for some the open acceptance of homosexuality in Ancient Greek culture was treasured as the kind of liberation which could only be dreamed of in England at that time. The romantic overtones of the struggle for Greek independence in the 19th century would also have played in Vita and Harold's minds, for that cause was mixed up with Lord Byron and the wider Romantic movement. And there was a family connection as well. Harold's grandmother's grandfather had taken from Delos five marble 'altars' – supposedly used for sacrifice, though they actually resemble column bases. The idea was that they would be prominently positioned in this garden. (One of them was made into the Shanganagh column which now sits in the Orchard.)

Delos remained in a state of suspended animation from 1970 until 2019, when the National Trust embarked on a restoration project aimed at reinstating the feature in a viable form. The garden designer Dan Pearson, retained as a consultant at Sissinghurst since 2014, collaborated with the then head gardener Troy Scott Smith to come up with a planting plan that could work. One Sissinghurst gardener was despatched to Delos to research the landscape and flora. The soil was altered and augmented and made much more free-draining (it is now 50 per cent grit), a wall was built around the site and certain trees were taken away so that more light could get in (the removal of an old oak on the Dartmouth Lawn was a controversial decision). This more open aspect was also a response to Vita and Harold's desire to create 'sea views' of the surrounding countryside in homage to the Delian maritime landscape.

Large boulders were levered into place in the autumn of 2019, and positioned to resemble the stones in Harold and Vita's photographs of Delos, taken in 1935. These boulders, which come from a Kentish rag-stone quarry 16 kilometres/10 miles away, have a suitably light

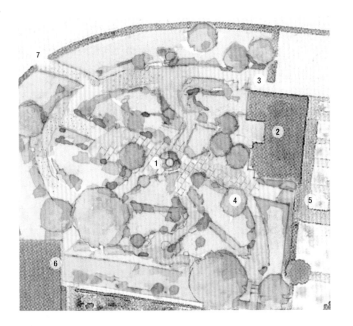

DELOS RESTORED

Sissinghurst's 'godparent', garden designer Dan Pearson, was in 2019 asked to redesign Delos in sympathetic but practical spirit. The layout has been altered but the original principle of five distinct areas has been retained.

KEY
1. Well
2. Priest's House
3. Exit to North Garden and Orchard
4. Pomegranate tree and altar
5. Entrance from White Garden
6. Entrance from Top Courtyard
7. Exit to Dartmouth Lawn

and dusty look. Vita and Harold's original ground plan was not followed; instead a central 'avenue' of dressed stone has been made, cutting east-west across from the White Garden to an exit to the Dartmouth Lawn. The idea of five separate areas of boulders divided by paths has been retained, though to a different layout, with one path now linking Delos with the Top Courtyard as well. The aim was not to make a 'rock garden' but a recreation of a natural landscape and plant community. Harold's altars have been set around the space, along with a small classical capital which was formerly in the Herb Garden.

The flat terraces have been tilted slightly towards the south, against the natural gradient, to maximise exposure to sunlight. Several benches and rocks for 'perching' have also been added. There is a well at the centre and, near the Priest's House, one of the altars creates a focus, shaded by a pomegranate tree. One last job earmarked for 2020 was the removal of the garage building north of the Priest's House – to enable visitors to progress from Delos directly into the little North Garden, and from there either into the White Garden or up through the boathouse and on into the Orchard.

Trees and large shrubs were the first plants to go in: cork oaks, pomegranate, fig, almond and arbutus. The shrub mix includes various kinds of cistus, phillyreas, *Sarcopoterium spinosum*, pistacia, rhamnus and the smaller olive *Olea europaea* 'Cipressino', with support from lavenders, thymes, rosemaries (including *Rosmarinus × mendizabalii*) and myrtles. No fewer than nine different phlomis have been planted in the garden, along with salvias, teucrium and dianthus, coronilla and euphorbias. More decorative perennial 'border' plants include achilleas (*Achillea coarctata*, *A. crithmifolia*, *A. umbellata*), linarias, *Centaurea bella*, *Verbascum olympicum*, *Delphinium*

RIGHT: Vinca minor *(above)* and Viburnum tinus *(below) number among the tough plants deployed in Delos.*

staphisagria, the very blue *Eryngium amethystinum*, *Iris lazica* and *I. unguicularis* 'Lucien', and the crimson peony, *Paeonia peregrina*. These are not arranged as border plants, but have been dispersed so that as far as possible they mimic how they might grow in the wild. The 'maquis' plants of the region will perhaps contribute most to the atmosphere and include subjects such as *Sideritis cypria*, *S. syriaca*, *Inula verbascifolia*, *Sedum sediforme*, *Stachys cretica* and various oreganos, along with a handful of perennial grasses, such as *Melica ciliata* and *Stipa barbata*.

One of the most interesting aspects of the garden is the emphasis on annuals raised from seed (some of it collected directly from Delos). Most are wild flowers, such as the dramatic *Trifolium stellatum*, bright purple *Legousia pentagonia* and the blue lupine, *Lupinus pilosus*. Other interesting annuals include *Fumaria capreolata*: the white ramping fumitory with exquisite, purple-tipped flowers; unusual *Crupina cruprinastrum*; and the vivid little pink *Silene cretica*. Less demonstrative are pale flax (*Linum bienne*) and soft mauve *Knautia integrifolia* (grown from Delos seed). Of bulbous plants, there are several hundred each of *Galanthus elwesii*, *Crocus sativus*, *C. pulchellus*, *Narcissus tazetta*, *Sternbergia lutea*, *Cyclamen coum* and *Scilla hyacinthoides*. Large numbers of native Mediterranean annual grasses (eight different species) are also being grown from seed, so that visitors may for a moment believe they are on a Greek island, as opposed to a corner of Kent.

The renewed Delos adds yet another flavour to Sissinghurst, a fragment of Vita and Harold's imaginations through which they can still communicate with us to this day. Delos represents one last moment of transformation in a garden that operates as a succession of dreamlike episodes and intimacies – drawing the visitor in and casting a spell that will often last a lifetime. 🦋

RIGHT: At the heart of Delos sits one of Harold's Greek 'altars', shaded by a gnarled pomegranate tree.

Envoi

A Summer's Evening at Sissinghurst Turns into Night

the brick liquefies

soft like a cake
crept across by
spindle thorns

drowsy petals
nodding and lolling

come on through
no one is here
scuffing your shoes
on the brick and flags
down the little hill
four yew trees and
into the roses

you can feel
the warmth of the
last of the crowds
departed

the old oaks sit tight
above the hedges
and the walls
the hedges
and the walls
make squares
and circles
which do not speak

the flowers speak

purple roses cluster
pink and red
yellow and white
perched on posts
daring spectators
singing with
the operatic lilies
and above them
the clematis in mid-air
holding aloof
murmuring their
serious comportment

flowers crowd round
the roses hanging
plumes of hesperis
tingling in the breeze
bending foxgloves
weighed down with
treasure of nectar
riot-police acanthus
advancing
over hedges
surrounded by
unreal pinks
mournful campanulas
the black poppies
dying every day

just a little more
purple to black
and back again
and everywhere
the going over
and gone-over roses

here they are again
pink roses frothing
like waves in the
cow parsley foam
the sudden surging
spikes of the foxtails
matronly lupins
in lemon cream
and behind the box hedges
lie coral reefs or
underwater treasure
the popping up seedpods
of alliums and iris
sweet peas bundling
themselves in
knots all
twisted and
turned and
then there is
the tower

what delicacies are here

the irises are
organising them-
selves making them-
selves respectable

annabelle has no idea
how beautiful she is

the roses tremble
lemon cephalaria
quivering in cobwebs
of smoking fennel
hostas lurk
like submarines
in the gloaming
and those wood pigeons
are opening up again

look up and see
the sky
the simple sky

the limes
their sturdy
trunks stock still
like the legs
of fat boys

above the hornbeam
sweet peas peeping

and the blue sky
is converted
to soft grey

slip away
slip away
into scintillation
dahlias like plump cushions
the lilies sweet and rich
kniphofias twiddling
verbascums upright
phloxes hoarding
the fading light
and the yews secret
as the sea

there is no celebrity now
in the curious cottage
only corydalis
sprouting from the cracks

out into the trees
the low trees
where balls of light
haphazardly bombard
the leaning bundled
sheaves and stems

the clamorous leaves

a blackbird twitching
on the mulch

sunlit hangers
beyond hidden lakes
a throne in the herb room
a herb in the throne room
the thyme bubbling
as the birds sing
of sadness and solace

the oak tree leaves
curl up towards the light

a duck plashes
delicately into the moat
to no interest from
the languid staring statue

the clouds conspire still
with the trees but
the sky is turning iron

young apples with
hard little red faces
sit tight on their stalks
dormers spy
the sad orchard
and the bell in the tower
is chiming again
and everything
swells and recedes

hedges stretched
between the walls
the tautness of
the court
wind blowing
through the gate
the bronze uneven
steps stand
to attention
the birds are
staggering around
seedheads bobble and
glow like asteroids
cardoons mingle
with the brick
and there are plenty
of conversations
at lights-out despite
that overbearing magnolia

startled by whiteness
at last
a splintered iceberg
detached
unmoored
from the universe
unpent and released
falling into its
pinpoints and tangles
sprinklings
layerings
cropping out the box
with its silver heart
still and not still
contained and released
those lilies yearning
for ever and ever
my mind is white my
head is white my
mouth is white
and the petals fall
one by one
over the yew walk
and on to the urn

this garden breaks me

the orchard lies down
for the night

the sun falls in

the garden collapses

barred gates and
dark lanes
are forgotten

the birds move in
over the misting woods
discarded garlands

lie on the thick grass
the nut trees start to glow
plants muster and mass
flowers stiffen
scent grows thicker
as the chill descends

the tower seems taller
in the night's start

true dusk is crisis

the garden suspended
weightless
obscured
how can it survive one night

I hardly dare
enter in again
standing on the threshold
then one step down
the spell is not broken but
I think I may be dead

the fennel is floating
in burgundy and gilt
the roses and foxgloves
have disappeared

the lilies are clustering

they are angels glowing
unto the last

— O —

A stream-of-consciousness poem
composed at Sissinghurst Castle
1 July 2019

                    Tim Richardson

Index

Picture Credits

Page 8 © The Cecil Beaton Studio Archive at Sotheby's

Pages 39, 42–3, 47, 48–49, 53 (top), 55, 60–61, 144 © National Trust/Rachel Warne

Pages 68–9 © National Trust/Andrew Butler

Page 119 © National Trust/Marianne Majerus

Page 158 © National Trust/Jonathan Buckley

Page 169 © National Trust/David Dixon

Acknowledgments

Acknowledgments from Tim Richardson

My thanks, first of all, to Troy Scott Smith, who was head gardener at Sissinghurst when I embarked on this book. He has been my main point of contact with the garden and has been unfailingly helpful throughout, while his deep knowledge of the garden has been invaluable. His successor, Michelle Cain, who took over just as the book was nearing completion, has been equally hospitable. I would like to thank Dan Pearson for writing the Foreword and for his insights into the garden. I would also like to thank Linda Davies, plants database volunteer at Sissinghurst, for her assistance.

It has been a privilege to work with photographer Jason Ingram. Rachel Warne kindly contributed supplementary photographs.

In addition to the books on the garden and its makers mentioned in the Introduction, may I gratefully acknowledge: *Vita and Virginia* (1993) by Suzanne Raitt; *Romantic Moderns* (2010) by Alexandra Harris; *Bloomsbury Rooms* (2004) by Christopher Reed; *Bloomsbury, Modernism, and the Reinvention of Intimacy* (2011) by Jesse Wolfe; *In the Hollow of the Wave: Virginia Woolf and Modernist Uses of Nature* (2012) by Bonnie Kime Scott; and *A Shrinking Island: Modernism and National Culture in England* (2004) by Jed Esty. An unpublished research report on the White Garden, undertaken for the NT by Monique Wolak, has been a useful source of information. The Royal Horticultural Society *Encyclopedia of Roses* by Charles Quest-Ritson has been the 'bible' for the genus, with redoubled thanks to the author for helping to clear up a few late queries. I would like to thank Michael Hall for reading the manuscript and making judicious suggestions, and Anthony Noel, who has known the garden intimately for decades. I would like to thank the family – Juliet Nicolson, and Adam Nicolson and Sarah Raven – for their hospitality at the garden over the years, and for their help with various queries.

My thanks to the production team at Frances Lincoln: Helen Griffin as editorial director, designer Rachel Cross, and Zia Allaway for her work in the final stages. At Quarto, I would like to thank Richard Green for his support of the book, and Nicky Hill. My special thanks go to Sarah Higgens who, as copy-editor, has once again excelled in terms of attention to detail and sensitivity towards the text.

Acknowledgments from Jason Ingram

As with all good books there are always so many people to thank. Firstly, I would like to thank Helen Griffin of Frances Lincoln for commissioning me to shoot this book and Tim Richardson for his words. I also want to thank The National Trust and all the gardeners at Sissinghurst for their hospitality, support and constant monitoring of the gardens, thereby enabling me to always be there at the right time. A special thanks to Troy Scott Smith for showing me the finer details of the garden and meeting me at sunrise on numerous occasions, and finally to our editor Zia Allaway and designer Rachel Cross, who I have worked with in selecting images for the book, as well as captioning and making them look so beautiful on the pages.

Sissinghurst's head gardeners

Tom and George Hayter (gardeners) 1930–36; Gordon Farley 1936–39; Jack Vass 1939–57; Ronald Platt 1957–59; Pamela Schwerdt and Sibylle Kreutzberger 1959–90; Sarah Cook 1990–2004; Alexis Datta 2004–13; Troy Scott Smith 2013–19; Michelle Cain 2019 onwards.